Eleventh Hour Network+

Exam N10-004 Study Guide

Syngress Eleventh Hour Series

Eleventh Hour Linux+: Exam XK1-003 Study Guide
ISBN: 978-1-59749-497-7
Graham Speake

Eleventh Hour Security+: Exam SYO-201 Study Guide
ISBN: 978-1-59749-427-4
Ido Dubrawsky

Eleventh Hour Network+: Exam N10-004 Study Guide
ISBN: 978-1-59749-428-1
Naomi Alpern

Eleventh Hour Network+
Exam N10-004 Study Guide

Naomi J. Alpern

Robert J. Shimonski

Technical Editor
Matthew Shepherd

ELSEVIER

AMSTERDAM • BOSTON • HEIDELBERG • LONDON
NEW YORK • OXFORD • PARIS • SAN DIEGO
SAN FRANCISCO • SINGAPORE • SYDNEY • TOKYO

Syngress is an imprint of Elsevier

SYNGRESS.

Syngress is an imprint of Elsevier
30 Corporate Drive, Suite 400, Burlington, MA 01803, USA
Linacre House, Jordan Hill, Oxford OX2 8DP, UK

Eleventh Hour Network+ Exam N10-004 Study Guide
Copyright © 2010 Elsevier Inc. All rights reserved.

Notices
Knowledge and best practice in this field are constantly changing. As new research and experience broaden our understanding, changes in research methods, professional practices, or medical treatment may become necessary.

Practitioners and researchers must always rely on their own experience and knowledge in evaluating and using any information, methods, compounds, or experiments described herein. In using such information or methods they should be mindful of their own safety and the safety of others, including parties for whom they have a professional responsibility.

To the fullest extent of the law, neither the Publisher nor the authors, contributors, or editors, assume any liability for any injury and/or damage to persons or property as a matter of products liability, negligence or otherwise, or from any use or operation of any methods, products, instructions, or ideas contained in the material herein.

Library of Congress Cataloging-in-Publication Data
Application submitted

British Library Cataloguing-in-Publication Data
A catalogue record for this book is available from the British Library.

ISBN: 978-1-59749-428-1

Working together to grow
libraries in developing countries

www.elsevier.com | www.bookaid.org | www.sabre.org

ELSEVIER   BOOK AID International   Sabre Foundation

Contents

Authors

Naomi J. Alpern currently works for Microsoft as a consultant specializing in Unified Communications. She holds many Microsoft certifications, including an MCSE and MCT, as well as additional industry certifications such as Citrix Certified Enterprise Administrator, Security+, Network+, and A+. Since the start of her technical career, she has worked in many facets of the technology world, including IT administration, technical training, and, most recently, full-time consulting. She likes to spend her time reading cheesy horror and mystery novels when she isn't browsing the Web. She is also the mother of two fabulous boys, Darien and Justin, who mostly keep her running around like a headless chicken.

Robert J. Shimonski (MCSE) is an entrepreneur, a technology consultant, and a published author with over 20 years of experience in business and technology. Robert's specialties include designing, deploying, and managing networks, systems, virtualization, storage-based technologies, and security analysis. Robert also has many years of diverse experience deploying and engineering mainframes and Linux- and Unix-based systems such as Red Hat and Sun Solaris. Robert has in-depth work-related experience with and deep practical knowledge of globally deployed Microsoft- and Cisco-based systems and stays current on the latest industry trends. Robert consults with business clients to help forge their designs, as well as to optimize their networks and keep them highly available, secure, and disaster-free.

Robert was the technical editor for and a contributing author to *Sniffer Pro Network Optimization & Troubleshooting Handbook* (ISBN: 978-1-931836-57-9, Syngress), the technical editor for *Security+ Study Guide and DVD Training System* (ISBN: 978-1-931836-72-2, Syngress), lead author and technical editor for *Network+ Study Guide & Practice Exams: Exam N10-003* (ISBN: 978-1-931836-42-5, Syngress), and technical editor for and a contributing author to *Building DMZs for Enterprise Networks* (ISBN: 978-1-931836-88-3, Syngress). Robert was most recently a contributing author to *Microsoft Vista for IT Security Professionals* (ISBN: 978-1-59749-139-6), a contributing author to *The Real MCTS/MCITP Configuring Microsoft Windows Vista Client Exam 70-620 Prep Kit* (ISBN: 978-1-59749-233-1, Syngress), and technical reviewer for *The Real MCTS/MCITP Windows Server 2008 Configuring Active Directory Exam 70-640 Prep Kit* (ISBN: 978-1-59749-235-5, Syngress). Robert can be found online at www.shimonski.com.

Technical Editor

Matthew Shepherd (CISSP, MCSE, MCDBA, GCFW, CEH) is a consultant in the Security and Privacy Division at Project Performance Corporation in McLean, VA. Matt uses his experience as a network administrator, IT manager, and security architect to deliver high-quality solutions for Project Performance Corporation's clients in the public and private sector. Matt holds bachelor's degrees from St. Mary's College of Maryland, and he is currently working on his master's of science in information assurance.

Matt would like to thank his wife, Leena, for her wonderful support during this project and throughout their relationship. He thanks his family for a lifetime of love and support and Olive for making every day special.

CHAPTER 1

Network Fundamentals

Exam objectives in this chapter
- What Is a Network?
- Logical Network Topologies
- Physical Network Topologies
- Network Types

WHAT IS A NETWORK?

The basic concept of networking is the difference between standing alone and being part of a group. Computers can also be standalone or part of a network. Networks are the systems that interconnect computers and other devices and provide a method of communication and the capability to share data.

Fast Facts

A computer network exists when two or more machines are connected together, thereby allowing them to share data, equipment, and other resources. By using a combination of software and hardware, the computers gain added functionality, including the capability to

- transfer data between machines
- save and access files on the same hard disks or other storage devices
- share printers, scanners, modems, and other peripheral devices
- allow messages to be exchanged via e-mail, instant messaging, and other technologies.

Network Elements

Although networks may provide similar functions, they can be very different. Some of the elements that will define your network and make it different from others include the following:

- **Network interface cards** (NIC) or **network adapters** allow computers to transmit and receive data across the network; *routers*, *switches*, and *hubs* pass the data to other computers or networks.
- **Media** consist of cables or wireless technologies that carry the data across the network.
- **Protocols** are sets of rules that control how the data is sent between computers. The most popular of these is the protocol used on the Internet, Transmission Control Protocol/Internet Protocol (TCP/IP), while other protocols used on networks include Internetwork Packet Exchange/Sequenced Packet Exchange (IPX/SPX) and AppleTalk.
- **Topology** is the shape of the network. It defines how the network is designed and describes how computers are connected together.
- **Network type** defines the size of the network and its scale within a geographical area.
- **Network model** determines the levels of security that are available to the network and the components needed to connect the computers together.
- **Access** determines who can use the network and how, and if features of the network are available for private or public use.
- **Network operating systems** (NOSes), such as Windows, NetWare, and Linux, may be used for a server, which is a computer that provides services to numerous computers, and/or installed on computers that are used by individual users of the network. In some cases, such as Novell NetWare, additional software may need to be installed on computers that use the server, who are referred to as clients.
- **Other software and services,** such as whether the network provides access to internal Web sites, e-mail, databases, and so forth, are also included in the network.

Networks may use different protocols, topologies, and other elements that make them unique. This means you can look at two networks in two different homes or businesses, and they can be completely different from one another. However, because the same basic set of protocols, topologies, media, and other elements are used to build these networks, they will all have similarities.

LOGICAL NETWORKING TOPOLOGIES

There are different network models that can be chosen. The network model you choose will affect a network infrastructure's design and how it is administered. The model or models used can have an impact on the location of computers, how users access resources, and the number of computers and types of operating systems required. Some models and topologies available to choose from are as follows:

- Centralized
- Decentralized (distributed)
- Peer-to-peer
- Client/server
- Virtual private network (VPN)
- Virtual local area network (VLAN)

Selecting a network model is the first important step in completing a network design. Another important decision involves determining how resources will be accessed. Centralized, decentralized, or a mixture of both are possible choices.

Centralized

When a centralized network model is used, a network's resources are centrally located and administered.

Here are the key points about centralized network models that you should know:

- A centralized model will affect the physical location of servers and other resources on your network by situating them within a specific area.
- Servers are generally located in a secure, central location, such as a dedicated server room. This secured room can also be used to house other resources, such as routers, switches, firewalls, Web servers, and other devices.
- The centralized network model can also mean that fewer servers or other devices are needed. Rather than each building having their own server on the premises, users can save their work to a dedicated server in a central location. This would keep everyone's files on one or more servers, allowing their work to be kept secure and regularly backed up.

DID YOU KNOW?

Additional work may be required to manage devices stored in a central location. For example, let's say you had a plotter that was kept in a server room. Anytime anyone needed the plotter installed as a printer on his or her computer, you would need to set up permissions on the plotter granting them usage rights. If the user sent a print job to this plotter, someone from the IT staff would need to enter the secure room to get the user's printout. In addition, there would also be the need to replace paper and toners used in the device. In a centralized model, administration of the resources is also centralized.

Despite the scenario described in the preceding sidebar, in some ways, managing resources can be easier with this model. By keeping these resources in one area, a network administrator can easily change backup tapes, replace hard disks, or fix other issues as required. Imagine the issues of having servers in offices throughout a city or region and having to visit each of them whenever a tape needed to be replaced after a tape backup. By keeping resources centralized, administrative work can be reduced.

Decentralized (Distributed)

When a decentralized network model is used, a network's resources are distributed through different areas of the network, and administration is shared by designating responsibility to system administrators or individual users.

Here are the key points about decentralized network models that you should know:

- A decentralized network model has a variety of servers, equipment, and other resources distributed across the geographical area making up the network, which aren't readily physically accessible. Cost factors or other issues may influence the requirement for a decentralized network.
- Distributing servers may improve network performance since users would no longer have to authenticate across wide area network (WAN) links or use slow connections to access remote servers.

Peer-to-Peer

In a peer-to-peer network, computers on the network are equal, with each workstation providing access to resources and data. This is a simple type of network where computers are able to communicate with one another and share what is on or attached to their computer with other users. It is also one of the easiest types of architectures to create. Here are some of the characteristics of a peer-to-peer network:

- Individual users have responsibility over who can access data and resources on their computers.
- Operating systems such as Windows XP and Windows Vista allow accounts to be set up that will be used when other users connect to an individual user's computer.
- Accounts, passwords, and permissions are saved in a local database and are used to determine what someone can do when connecting to your computer.

DID YOU KNOW?

One important issue with peer-to-peer networks is security. Each computer on this type of network may allow or deny access to other computers, as access to data and resources is controlled on each machine. For example, a user could share a folder containing payroll information on his or her computer, allowing other users to access the files in that folder. Because users can control access to files and resources on their computers, network administration isn't controlled by one person. As such, peer-to-peer networks are generally used in small deployments and in situations where security isn't a major concern, as in the case of home networks or small businesses.

> **EXAM WARNING**
>
> A peer-to-peer network is decentralized, because resources and administration are handled locally on each participating machine, while a client/server network can be either centralized or decentralized. Remember the differences and relationships between different network types for the exam, as they may be covered either directly or incorporated in the scenarios used to cover other material.

Client/Server

When you use a peer-to-peer network model, each machine can house data and also request data from other machines, so the computers act as both clients and servers, depending on the action performed. In a client/server network, model machines have a distinct role. Here are some characteristics of the client/server model:

- Roles are distinct since the client/server model involves dedicated servers that provide services and data, and dedicated clients, which do not house data content.
- The client/server model consists of high-end computers serving clients on a network, by providing specific services upon request.
- Each server may perform a single role, or a mixture of roles can be combined on a single server machine.

Crunch Time

Examples of various client/server roles include the following:

- **File server** allows clients to save data to files and folders on its hard drive.
- **Print server** redirects print jobs from clients to specific printers.
- **Application server** allows clients to run certain programs on the server and enables multiple users to common applications across the network.
- **Database server** allows authorized clients to view, modify, and/or delete data in a common database.

- The server needs to have an NOS like Windows Server 2003, Windows Server 2008, or Linux installed.
- These server operating systems provide features specifically for servicing clients and can respond more efficiently to a greater number of client requests than operating systems intended for client roles such as Windows XP or Windows Vista.
- Once a high-end computer has server software installed, the services provided by it need to be configured and other programs may need to be installed.
- Many of the server's functions are dependent on the server software installed on it. For example, a server that acts as a database server needs to have a

program like Microsoft SQL Server or mySQL installed on it. In the same way, a Windows Server 2008 server which must act as a Web server would need Internet Information Services (IIS) configured.

- By installing server software on the dedicated server, you define the role that the server will play on your network.

Virtual Private Network

A VPN provides users with a secure method of connectivity through a public network, such as the Internet, into the internal network of an organization. Most companies use dedicated connections to connect to remote sites. However, when users want to connect to that same corporate network from home over the Internet, it is important to consider security and require the additional security offered by encryption of the data using a VPN. It may also make sense to connect a small branch office using a VPN, which would cost less than a dedicated connection.

WHAT IS A VPN?

When a VPN is implemented properly, it provides wide area security, reduces costs associated with traditional WANs, improves productivity, and improves support for users who telecommute. Cost savings are twofold. First, companies save money by using public networks such as the Internet instead of paying for dedicated circuits between remote offices. Second, telecommuters do not have to pay long-distance fees to connect into centrally-located, corporate remote access servers. They can simply dial into their local Internet service providers (ISPs) and create a virtual tunnel to the office. A tunnel is created by encapsulating a data packet inside another data packet and transmitting it over a public medium.

Crunch Time

Tunneling requires three different protocols:

- **Carrier Protocol** The protocol used by the network (IP on the Internet) that the information is traveling over.

- **Encapsulating Protocol** The protocol, such as Point-to-Point Tunneling Protocol (PPTP), Layer 2 Tunneling Protocol (L2TP), IPsec, or Secure Shell (SSH), that is wrapped around the original data.
- **Passenger Protocol** The original data being carried.

Essentially, there are two different types of VPNs: site-to-site and remote access.

- **Site-to-site VPNs** are normally established between corporate offices that are separated by a physical distance extending further than normal local area network (LAN) media covers.

- VPNs are available as software implementations such as Windows VPN, available on Windows 2003 and 2008.
- VPNs are available as hardware implementations which may be deployed on firewall devices such as Cisco PIX and Check Point.
- Common protocols associated with VPN transmission security include the following:
  - PPTP – a tunneling protocol used to establish a secure tunnel connection between two sites
  - L2TP – a tunneling protocol used to establish a secure tunnel connection between two sites
  - SSH – an encryption protocol used to secure data passing through the tunnel
  - IPSec – an encryption protocol used to secure data passing through the tunnel
  - Secure Sockets Layer/Transport Layer Security (SSL/TLS) – an encryption protocol used to secure data passing through the tunnel
- **Remote access VPN,** also known as a *private virtual dial-up network* (PVDN), differs from a site-to-site VPN in that end users are responsible for establishing the VPN tunnel between their workstation and their remote office.
  - Users connect to the Internet or an ESP through a point of presence (POP) using their particular VPN client software and then authenticate with the VPN server, usually by username and password.
  - Allows employees to transmit data to their home offices from any location.
  - Good solution choice for a company with many employees working in the field.

Virtual Local Area Network

VLANs allow network administrators to divide the network by designating certain switch ports as part of a logical network. While several computers or devices can be connected to the same physical network, they can all be separated logically through the use of a VLAN. Characteristics of VLANs are as follows:

- VLAN databases can provide important details to any individual who is trying to discern the logical breakup of the network.
- VLANs logically divide the network and affect the traffic and security of a switched network.
- VLANs are commonly used in the enterprise or corporate computing networks to segment networks.

PHYSICAL NETWORKING MODELS

The topology of a network is the physical layout of computers, hubs, routers, cables, and other components. It provides a map of where things are and how the network is configured.

While networks are unique, the topology of each network will share characteristics with other networks.

Crunch Time

Networks may use a single topology or a combination of any of the following topologies:

- Bus
- Star
- Ring

- Mesh
- Point-to-point
- Point-to-multipoint
- Hybrid
- Wireless

EXAM WARNING

You must be able to identify a topology based on either the description given or by looking at a picture of a topology. Make sure you know each of the topologies covered in this section and can identify them via diagrams. Figure 1.1 displays examples of some of the topologies.

The Bus Topology

All the computers in a bus topology are connected together using a single cable, which is called a *trunk, backbone,* or *segment*. Characteristics of a bus topology are as follows:

- Coaxial cable is commonly used for the trunk.
- The computers in a bus topology are attached to the cable segment using T-connectors.
- Because all these computers use the same cable, only one computer can send packets of data onto the network at a time.
- When a computer sends a packet of data onto the trunk, it is sent in both directions so that every computer on the network has the chance to receive it.
- When a computer listens to the network, any packets that aren't addressed to it are discarded, while any packets specifically sent to it are examined further.
- A broadcast is made when packets are destined for every computer on the network.
- To prevent data signals from staying on the cable indefinitely, the cable needs to be terminated at each end so electronic signals are absorbed when they reach the cable's end.
- Without termination, packets sent would bounce back-and-forth along the length of the cable causing the entire network to fail.

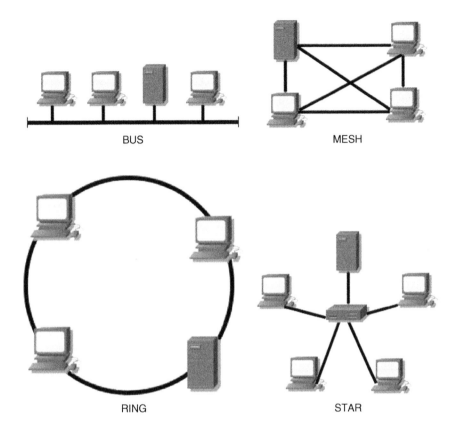

FIGURE 1.1
Sample network topologies

DID YOU KNOW?

In a bus topology, every computer is connected to a single cable. If the cable breaks, then each segment has an end that isn't terminated, and the entire network goes down. If the trunk is long enough, this can make it difficult to isolate where the break is.

Another disadvantage of this topology is that it isn't very scalable. The number of computers is limited to the length of the cable, and as your company grows, it can be difficult changing the size and layout of the network. Also, while changes or repairs are made to the cable, the network is down because there is no redundancy and termination of the cable is required.

The Star Topology (Hierarchical)

In a star topology, computers aren't connected to one another but are all connected to a central hub or switch. When a computer sends data to other computers on the network, it is sent along the cable to a central hub or switch, which then determines which port it needs to send the data through for it to reach the proper destination. Characteristics of a star topology are as follows:

- All cables run to a central connection point.
- If one cable breaks or fails, only the computer that is connected to that cable is unable to use the network.
- A star topology is scalable.
- As the network grows or changes, computers are simply added or removed from the central connection point, which is usually a hub or a switch.
- Because there is so much cabling used to connect individual computers to a central point, this may increase the cost of expanding and maintaining the network.

The Mesh Topology

A mesh topology has multiple connections, making it the most fault tolerant topology available. Every component of the network is connected directly to every other component. Characteristics of a mesh topology are as follows:

- A mesh topology provides redundant links across the network.
- If a break occurs in a segment of cable, traffic can still be rerouted using the other cables.
- This topology is rarely used because of the significant cost and work involved in having network components directly connected to every other component.
- It is common for partial mesh topologies to be deployed. This balances cost and the need for redundancy.

The Ring Topology

A ring topology consists of computers connected to a cable that loops around forming a ring. Characteristics of a ring topology are as follows:

- The topology forms a closed loop, so there are no unconnected ends to the ring, so terminators aren't required.
- Data passes around the loop in one direction.
- A signal called a *token* is passed from one computer to the next in the ring. When a computer has the token, it has access to the ring and can send data.
- Each computer examines each packet and checks to see if there are any that are meant for it. If there aren't, the computer sends the packet on to the next computer in the ring.
- Each computer acts as a repeater.
- When any packet reaches the originating computer, it removes the packet from the network.
- In a ring topology, if one computer fails, the entire network goes down.

- If a computer is down or a cable is broken, the ring can't be completed, so the network can't function properly.
- Some ring implementations have features that detect and disconnect failed computers from the ring or beacons that notify the network if a break is detected.

POINT-TO-POINT

A point-to-point topology is any network that connects two hosts in a dedicated fashion. For example, if you were to configure a router in Miami, Florida, to connect and use resources on a network in Atlanta, Georgia, you would want to make sure you had a link between them that can support your needs. If you need a permanent connection that is constantly available and dependable, you may need a T1 circuit. Although costly, you will be able to connect your two sites together resulting in a point-to-point connection that is dependable and reliable.

POINT-TO-MULTIPOINT

A point-to-multipoint topology is any network that connects three or more hosts and can grow exponentially based on the hardware and software you choose to manage it. For example, if you wanted to create a large network of many sites (that is, New York, Georgia, Florida and Michigan), you may need to create a point-to-multipoint network. The main connection could be your headquarters location, and the other three sites could be smaller sites accessing resources in the main "hub" site. This type of network is also called a *"hub-and-spoke"* topology.

HYBRID

A hybrid topology is any mixture of at least two or more of any network topologies. Most networks aren't purely configured as one type of topology but are deployed in some form of hybrid network.

Wireless

A wireless topology broadcasts data over the air, so very few cables are used to connect systems together.

Characteristics of radio frequency-based wireless environments are as follows:

- This topology uses transmitters called *cells*, which broadcast the packets using radio frequencies.
- The cells extend a radio sphere around the transmitter in the shape of a bubble that can extend to multiple rooms and possibly different floors in a building.
- Each cell is connected to the network using cabling so that it can receive and send data to the servers, other cells, and networked peripherals.

- Computers and other devices have a device installed in them that transmits and receives data to and from the cell, allowing them to communicate with the network.
- Wireless networks can also extend their transmission to wireless devices by implementing radio antennas that are situated on buildings or towers. The antenna serves as a cell that will cover a wider area, such as a building or campus.

Characteristics of infrared-based wireless environments are as follows:

- Infrared communications require a direct line of site and close proximity for the communication to work.
- This type of wireless networking is similar to using a remote control for a TV, where each device needs to be lined up and within range of one another.
- Because of its limitations, it isn't generally used for networking but may be seen in a networked environment for connecting laptops and other computers to devices like printers.

Here are some of the potential issues that may occur in wireless networks:

- There is a chance of transmissions being blocked or experiencing interference.
- Machinery and other devices can emit radio frequencies or electrical interference that disrupts signals being exchanged between the cell and wireless devices.
- Some buildings using cinderblocks, large amounts of metal, or insolated to prevent transmissions from interfering with equipment can keep a wireless network from working between rooms.

NETWORK TYPES

A network can be in a single building or comprising computers connected together over a broader geographical area. To categorize the scope of a network, different terms have been created to classify these different network types. The types of networks that could be created include the following:

- Local area network (LAN)
- Wide area network (WAN)
- Metropolitan area network (MAN)
- Storage area network (SAN)
- Personal area network (PAN)
- Campus area network (CAN)

Local Area Network and Wide Area Network

LANs and WANs were the first types of networks to be classified by the area they covered. Although each of the names refers to an area, an exact range has never been firmly established and is left vague. LANs are networks spanning a limited distance, whereas a WAN is a network that is larger than a LAN. The distance difference that distinguishes a LAN from a WAN in terms of area is ambiguous and speculative.

Characteristics of a LAN are as follows:

- LANs are small to medium-sized networks and generally connect network devices that are no more than a few miles of one another, which Institute of Electrical and Electronics Engineers, Inc. (IEEE) defines as being 4 km or less in diameter.
- LANs include networks that have been set up in homes, offices, the floor of a building, an entire building, a campus or group of nearby buildings, or facilities that are relatively close to one another.
- Typically, a LAN is owned by a single person or organization and is managed by a single person or group of people.

Characteristics of a WAN are as follows:

- WANs can span great geographical distances and connect different LANs together using high-speed solutions or telephone lines.
- A WAN may connect LANs in different cities, regions, states/provinces, or even countries.
- With WANs, ownership isn't a defining factor. WANs are often owned and managed by more than one organization.
- Each LAN that is part of the WAN may be managed by individuals or IT departments, and either the former or the latter maintains its connection to the rest of the LAN or hires outside parties to perform that function.

Crunch Time

An effective way of understanding how a local area network is related to a WAN is to look at how they are connected and how data is sent. This may differ from organization to organization, as there are several different ways of getting data from a LAN to a WAN, including the following:

- **Modem** is a device that allows you to connect to other computers and devices using telephone lines. Generally, when a modem is mentioned, it refers to a dial-up modem (as opposed to the digital modems used for other methods mentioned below). This type of connection is slow and allows connections at a maximum of 56 Kbps (meaning that 56,000 bits of data can be sent or received per second)
- **Integrated Services Digital Network (ISDN)** sends data over telephone lines but at higher speeds up to 128 Kbps but averaging at 64 Kbps using an ISDN modem or router.
- **Digital subscriber line (DSL)** sends data across telephone lines at speeds ranging from 1.5 million bits per second (Mbps) using a router or digital modem and configured phone lines.
- **Cable** transmits the data across cable lines using the same lines used for cable television at speeds of up to 1.5 Mbps.
- **Satellite** transmits data to a satellite at speeds of up to 400 Kbps.
- **T1 and T3** are dedicated connections that provide extremely high speeds. A T1 line provides speeds of 1.544 Mbps, while a T3 line provides speeds ranging from 3 Mbps to 44.736 Mbps

To illustrate the relationships between LANs and WANs, let's look at a situation that may be familiar to you: sending an e-mail to another person. Here is a general overview of the process:

1. Using the e-mail program on your home computer, you would address, compose, and send an e-mail message.
2. Your e-mail is sent to the network adapter, where it is broken up into smaller chunks called *packets* that can be sent more efficiently over the network.
3. These packets are transmitted over the connection in your home LAN to the router that is used to connect to the Internet.
4. The router examines the information pertaining to the packet's end destination, and the router determines if the destination is for a computer on the LAN or if the packets need to be sent to the ISP that provides your Internet connection.
5. Since in this case you're sending an e-mail to someone who isn't on your home network, the router would use the WAN connection between your LAN and the ISP's LAN to send the e-mail.
6. When the ISP receives your e-mail, it also looks at where the data is destined. Because the ISP also has a LAN, it looks at whether the e-mail is destined for someone else who uses their service, a computer on their network, or another network connected to the Internet.
7. Since you're sending the e-mail to someone who uses a different ISP, the e-mail is broken into packets and sent over the Internet, which is a giant WAN, to be received by the other ISP's e-mail server.
8. When the other ISP receives the data, it will store the e-mail you sent on its e-mail server, until your friend dials into the Internet using a modem.
9. Your friend's computer connects to the ISP's server and then requests any e-mail that the e-mail server might have.
10. This data is again broken into packets and sent over the telephone line so that your friend's modem can receive the data, and their computer can reassemble these packets and display them in your friend's e-mail program.

As you can see by this example, there are many different kinds of LANs and WANs that data may pass through. LANs may be as small as a couple of computers networked together, and a WAN may be as large as the Internet or as small as two LANs (yours and your ISP's) interconnected together using routers. In each case, the LAN consists of computers that are part of the same network and the WAN consists of geographically dispersed LANs that are internetworked.

Metropolitan Area Network

While most people refer to a network in terms of being either a LAN or a WAN, an additional category that exists is called a metropolitan area network (MAN). A MAN will generally cover a metropolitan area like a city, but this isn't always the case. When LANs are connected together with high-speed solutions over a territory that is relatively close together (such as several buildings in a city, region, or county), it can be considered a MAN. A MAN is a group of LANs that are internetworked within a local geographic area, which IEEE defines as being 50 km or less in diameter.

Storage Area Network

A SAN is used to connect storage devices together using high-speed connections. It is a segment of a network that allows storage devices to be accessed by computers within the larger LAN or WAN. These storage devices consist of hard disks or other methods of storing data and allow users of the network to view and/or save data to a centralized location.

Personal Area Network

A PAN is a wireless network that allows devices to exchange data with computers. Personal digital assistants (PDAs), cell phones, and other devices that someone can carry on their person and support this technology have a wireless transmitter in them. When they are within a certain distance of a receiver that's installed on a computer, data can be exchanged between the computer and the device. Using a PAN allows you to do such things as update a calendar in a PDA, address book in a cell phone, and other tasks that are supported by the device.

Campus Area Network

A CAN refers to a series of LANs that are internetworked between several nearby buildings. This is a common type of network that's used in organizations with facilities that are close to one another, such as when there is a pool of office buildings or a campus. It is larger than a LAN but smaller than a MAN.

Summary of Exam Objectives

We have reviewed the various network types, topologies, and models available for a network. A network can use a centralized or distributed model and be designed as a client/server model or peer-to-peer. In creating a network, you will use one or more topologies, which represents the physical layout of network components. The topologies we covered in this chapter were bus, star, ring, mesh, and wireless. Finally, the geographic scope of a network will determine what type of network you have. LANs are small networks within a limited area of a few miles, MANs are within a metropolitan area, and WANs interconnect LANs over a wide area. These characteristics define your network and will affect a wide variety of elements including security, media, and other features that make up your network as a whole.

Top Five Toughest Questions

1. A new intranet has been created in your organization, and it includes a File Transfer Protocol (FTP) site to download files and a news server for sharing information. The network is internetworked with a network belonging to a subsidiary of the company. The subsidiary's network uses Apple computers and uses AppleTalk as a network protocol. To access the intranet, which of the following protocols would need to be installed on your computer?
   A. IPX/SPX
   B. NWLink
   C. TCP/IP
   D. AppleTalk

2. Your company's network is on several floors of a building. Because of the amount of data being stored, there are three file servers, a Web server for the intranet, an e-mail server for internal e-mail, and an SQL Server that is used for several databases that have been developed in house. Because of security reasons, floppy disks and other devices to transfer or transmit data to and from the computer have been removed and aren't permitted. What type of network model is being used?
   A. Client/server
   B. Peer-to-peer
   C. MAN
   D. PAN

3. A company has multiple offices that are internetworked. Office A has a single computer that has the capability to dial into the Internet but isn't connected to the other offices. Office B is in another part of the country from the other offices but doesn't have its network interconnected to the other offices. Offices C and D are in separate states but have a dedicated connection between them. Office C has 20 computers that access each other's machines and provide services and data to one another. Office D has 50 computers that log onto the network using a single server. Based on this information, which of the Offices are part of a LAN and a WAN?
   A. Offices A and B
   B. Offices B and C
   C. Offices C and D
   D. The entire network (Offices A, B, C, and D)

4. You receive a call that the network is down. In this network, all the computers are connected together using a single cable, which they are connected to using T-connectors. Looking at the situation, you find that there is no break through the trunk. Which of the following is most likely the cause of the problem?
   A. A failed network card
   B. One of the computers is turned off
   C. T-connectors are missing from the ends of the cable
   D. Terminators are missing from the ends of the cable

5. Your network has 10 computers that are networked together using a star topology. Which of the following is a possible point of failure for this topology that could bring down the entire network?
A. Cable
B. Network card
C. T-connector
D. Hub

Answers

1. Correct answer and explanation: **C.** TCP/IP. Intranets use the same technologies as the Internet, which uses TCP/IP. To access an intranet using a Web browser, and fully take advantage of the services it provides, you would need to have TCP/IP installed just as you would if you were going to access the Internet.

Incorrect answers and explanations: **A**, **B**, and **D**. Answer **A** is incorrect because IPX/SPX is a protocol used on Novell NetWare networks but isn't a protocol that's used to access Internet sites (such as FTP sites that require TCP/IP). Although IPX/SPX was a default protocol for NetWare, recent versions use TCP/IP as a default protocol. Answer **B** is incorrect for similar reasons, as NWLink is an IPX/SPX compatible protocol that's used by Microsoft operating systems to connect to NetWare networks. Answer **C** is incorrect because AppleTalk is used for Apple networks but isn't the protocol used by various Internet technologies (such as FTP Sites).

2. Correct answer and explanation: **A**. Client/server. A decentralized network model has network resources and administration distributed throughout the network. Administration is shared by designating responsibility to system administrators or individual users, while resources such as servers and other devices are installed at various locations throughout the network. By sharing administrative burdens in this way, certain resources can now be managed by other members of the organization.

Incorrect answers and explanations: **B, C,** and **D**. Answer **B** is incorrect because servers are being used, so this isn't a peer-to-peer network. On a peer-to-peer network, computers on the network are equal and aren't in the role of dedicated servers. Answers **C** and **D** are incorrect because these aren't network models and are types of networks. Because the network doesn't extend across a metropolitan area, it isn't a MAN, and because personal devices aren't being used to network with computers or other network devices, it isn't a PAN.

3. Correct answer and explanation: **C**. Offices C and D. Both these offices have LANs. Office C has a peer-to-peer network, while Office D has a client\server network. They are interconnected to one another and thereby part of a WAN.

Incorrect answers and explanations: **A, B,** and **D**. Answer **A** is incorrect because Office A doesn't have a network but only an Internet connection.

It is also wrong because Office B isn't part of a WAN. Answer **B** is incorrect because although it has a LAN, it isn't connected to the other networks and therefore isn't part of the WAN. Answer **D** is incorrect because not every office has a LAN, and the others connected together form a WAN.

4. Correct answer and explanation: **D.** Terminators are missing from the ends of the cable. The topology described in the question refers to a bus topology and states that the entire network is down although there is no cable break. Terminators are needed on a bus topology because they prevent packets from bouncing up and down the cable. Terminators need to be attached to each end of the cable to absorb electronic signals. This clears the cable to allow other computers to send packets on the network. If there is no termination, the entire network fails.

   Incorrect answers and explanations: **A**, **B**, and **C.** Answer **A** is incorrect because a failed network card would only affect one computer. Answer **B** is incorrect because a bus topology is passive and doesn't require each computer to be present to receive and resend data along the cable. Answer **C** is incorrect because T-connectors are used to connect the computers to the cable. They aren't used to terminate the ends of a cable.

5. Correct answer and explanation: **D.** Hub. In a star topology, all computers are connected through one central hub. Computers are cabled to this hub making it a centralized point where the network is connected. If the hub fails, the network would go down.

   Incorrect answers and explanations: **A**, **B**, and **C.** Answer **A** is incorrect because if a cable broke or failed in some way, it would only remove the computer connected to it from the network. Answer **B** is incorrect because a failed network card in a computer would only prevent that particular computer from being able to access the network. Answer **C** is incorrect because a T-connector is used to connect computers to a cable in a bus topology. A star topology is being used in this situation.

CHAPTER 2
Network Media

Exam objectives in this chapter

- Cabling and Connectors Overview
- Media Issues
- Cable Testers and Troubleshooting
- Simplex, Half-Duplex, and Full Duplex
- Cabling
- Cable Management
- LAN Technologies and Media Standards
- Connectors
- Recognizing Cables

CABLING AND CONNECTORS OVERVIEW

The media that carry data make up the basic infrastructure of a network. Connectors provide an access point for data and are attached to the ends of the cables, which are plugged into a network card. This creates a physical link between each device and others on your network. Some cables can carry the data for 100 m or so, while others can span greater distances connecting widely dispersed systems. There are different types of cabling and different types of connectors that may be used.

Fundamentals of Cabling

The following are the three types of physical media that can be used on a network:

- Coaxial cable
- Twisted-pair cable
- Fiber-optic cable

DID YOU KNOW?

Coaxial cable contains a single copper wire at the center of the cable core that is used to carry the signals. Coaxial cable is surrounded by layers of insulation that protect the wire and its transmissions. There are two coaxial types:

- **Thinnet (10Base2)** Thinnet cable is 0.25 in. thick and is often used to connect endpoints to the backbone of a network.
- **Thicknet (10Base5)** Thicknet cable is 0.5 in. thick and is often used as a network backbone since the thicker cable allows for increased speeds and distances.

Twisted-pair cable is a type of cabling that's used for telephone and network communications. Twisted-pair cables have one or more pairs of copper wires that are insulated and twisted around one another, which prevent the signals on the wires from interfering with one another. Twisted-pair cabling may be shielded or unshielded. Two twisted-pair types:

- Unshielded twisted pair (UTP)
- Shielded twisted pair (STP) has an extra layer of aluminum/polyester between the wire and the plastic covering. This layer acts as a shield against interference from outside sources that could corrupt data carried on the copper wire.

To transmit data, fiber-optic cables use glass or plastic to transmit light pulses across the network. Because the information is transmitted at the speed of light, it can carry more information faster than other types of cabling.

Fundamentals of Connectors

Connectors are used to hold the ends of the wires or fibers in a cable in place, so that it can then be plugged into a network card or other equipment on your network. These connectors may be plastic or metal, and differ greatly in appearance.

Fast Facts

There are several different kinds of connectors that may be used with the different types of cabling, including the following:

- **Bayonet-Neill-Concelman (BNC)** This is a type of locking connector used to terminate coaxial cables. BNC is also known by many other names such as Bayonet Nut Connector, British Naval Connector, or Barrel Nut Connector.

- **Registered jack (RJ)** This is used with twisted-pair cables. RJ-11 is used for phone cables, while RJ-45 is a twisted-pair connector that is commonly used in networks.

- **Standard connector (SC)** This is used with fiber-optic cabling.

- **Straight tip (ST)** This is used with fiber-optic cabling.

- **Local connector (LC)** This is used with fiber-optic cabling.
- **Mechanical transfer registered jack (MTRJ)** This is used with fiber-optic cabling.

These different types of connectors attach a cable to network cards and other devices in different ways. Some connectors, like RJ-11, RJ-45, and ST connectors are plugged into a port, whereas others like BNC and ST connectors have threading that is used to screw the connector into place.

MEDIA ISSUES

Each of the different types of physical media available has its own benefits and vulnerabilities that can affect network performance and the amount of work required to install, troubleshoot, and repair the cabling.

Interference

Interference is an issue affecting media that transmit electrical signals such as UTP and coaxial cable. Fiber-optic cabling is not susceptible to interference since it is not a copper-based media and it uses light rather than electronic signals to transmit data. There are three main types of interference:

- **Electromagnetic interference (EMI)** It is a low voltage, low current, high frequency signal that comes from an outside source, which can interfere with the electronic signals transmitted over cabling. UTP is vulnerable, STP is less vulnerable, and fiber optic is immune to EMI.
- **Radio frequency interference (RFI)** It is caused by electromagnetic radiation in the radio frequency range generated by radio and television broadcast towers, microwave satellite dishes, appliances, and furnaces. UTP is vulnerable, STP is less vulnerable, and fiber optic is immune to RFI.
- **Crosstalk** The electromagnetic field of one wire interferes with the transmission of data along another wire. This type of interference can cause a loss or corruption of data. UTP is vulnerable, STP is less vulnerable, and fiber optic is immune to crosstalk.

> **EXAM WARNING**
>
> Don't get crosstalk confused with EMI. Remember that when one cable has its data communications bleed onto another cable, it is crosstalk. EMI can come from any number of sources, including florescent lights or machinery.

Bandwidth

Bandwidth is a measurement of the amount of data that can be passed over a cable in a given amount of time. The bandwidth capacity of a network cable is usually measured in the number of bits or bytes that can be transferred in a second. Table 2.1 shows the bandwidth capacity of different media standards.

Table 2.1	Bandwidth Capacity of Physical Media	
Media Standard	**Cable Type**	**Bandwidth Capacity**
10Base2	Coaxial	10 Mbps
10Base5	Coaxial	10 Mbps
10BaseT	UTP (Category 3 or higher)	10 Mbps
100BaseTX	UTP (Category 5 or higher)	100 Mbps
10BaseFL	Fiber optic	10 Mbps
100BaseFX	Fiber optic	100 Mbps
1000BaseT	UTP (Category 5 or higher)	1 Gbps (1000 Mbps)
1000BaseSX	Fiber optic	1 Gbps (1000 Mbps)
1000BaseLX	Fiber optic	1 Gbps (1000 Mbps)
1000BaseCX	Fiber optic	1 Gbps (1000 Mbps)
10GbaseSR	Fiber optic	10 Gbps
10GbaseLX4	Fiber optic	10 Gbps
10GbaseLR	Fiber optic	10 Gbps

If the amount of data exceeds the amount of bandwidth supported, the cabling can become a bottleneck.

Length Problems

As signals travel the length of a cable, it will weaken over distance resulting in signal degradation, which is called *attenuation*. Fiber-optic cabling doesn't suffer from attenuation as copper cabling does. Because attenuation can occur, it is important that you don't exceed the maximum distance of a cable. Table 2.2 shows the maximum lengths of various media standards.

Security Issues

The security of cabling should be considered before installing a particular kind of cabling. You will need to be aware of security issues that are inherent to certain types of cabling, such as

- **Wiretapping** This involves gaining physical access to a network cable and cutting or piercing the cable so that the wires inside the cable can be accessed and then spliced or tapped.
- **Eavesdropping** This involves listening to data being sent over the wire without actually piercing the cable.

Fiber-optic cabling is not susceptible to either of these vulnerabilities.

Table 2.2	Maximum Distance of Physical Media	
Media Standard	**Cable Type**	**Maximum Length**
10Base2	Coaxial	185 m
10Base5	Coaxial	500 m
10BaseT	UTP (Category 3 or higher)	100 m
100BaseTX	UTP (Category 5 or higher)	100 m
10BaseFL	Fiber optic	2 km
100BaseFX	Fiber optic	400 m (half-duplex) or 2 km (full duplex)
1000BaseT	UTP (Category 5 or higher)	100 m
1000BaseSX	Fiber optic	550 m (multimode fiber)
1000BaseLX	Fiber optic	550 m (multimode fiber) or up to 10 km (single mode fiber)
1000BaseCX	Fiber optic	100 m
10GbaseSR	Fiber optic	Up to 300 m over 2000 Mhz.km multimode fiber
10GbaseLX4	Fiber optic	Up to 10 km over single mode fiber
10GbaseLR	Fiber optic	Up to 10 km over single mode fiber

Installation

Twisted pair: UTP is thinner and more flexible than other types of cabling, making it easier to get around the corners, whereas STP is thicker than UTP, making it more rigid, which can make it more difficult to install around the corners. STP also requires an electrical ground with the connectors.

Coaxial cable: The connectors for coaxial cable are fairly simple to install, but the cable is relatively thick and rigid, and can require some finesse in navigating it around the corners.

Fiber optic: Installation and subsequent testing of fiber-optic cabling is difficult. Because glass or plastic is used to carry the data, connecting two pieces of cabling together can provide difficulties, as they must be fused together.

Troubleshooting

Cabling is one of the most common causes of network failure. Most often, the cable running from the workstation to the wall jack is the one that will be the problem. This is because the cable runs from central server room or telecom closets through walls are generally installed by technicians. These cables are hidden behind walls and ceilings, and are not exposed to the wear and tear of external cables. To troubleshoot cabling issues,

- Perform a visual inspection of cabling.
- Replace the cable with a known good cable, and retry the connection.
- Retest communications.
- Examine network interface card (NIC) to ensure connectivity.

Using tools that are designed for troubleshooting cable problems is another important factor in solving such problems quickly.

Crunch Time

Cable testers are tools that can analyze the capability of a cable to carry signals, and can find breaks or other problems in the wire. Examples of various *cable troubleshooting tools* include the following:

- **Tone generator (Fox and Hound)** This tool is used to perform tests and will aid in the identification of wires during the wire-tracing process. To use a tone generator, you begin by attaching the fox to the cable, jack, or panel that you would like to trace, and a signal is sent across a wire while you continue with the hound on the other end of the cable to find the fox's tone.
- **Time domain reflectometer (TDR)** This tool uses an electronic pulse, which travels down the cable until it is reflected back. The TDR then calculates the distance down the cable that the signal traveled before being reflected by measuring the amount of time it took for the signal to be returned. If this distance is less than your overall cable length, a cable problem exists at that distance from your location.
- **Wire map tester** This tool is used to test for opens, shorts, and crossed pairs, and will provide information that may indicate improper wiring. Because they are a low-cost cable tester, they generally provide fewer features than other cable testers, such as TDRs.

- **Oscilloscope** This tool can determine if there are shorts, crimps, or attenuation in the cable. An oscilloscope formats its output in a graphical format. Oscilloscopes are commonly used to test cables that have been recently run through walls to ensure there are no problems with the cable before using it.
- **Cable tester** This tool provides a variety of tests that can be performed on network cabling. The features of a handheld cable tester will vary, but some high-end testers will combine the features of several testers, such as providing the features of a wire map tester and a TDR or running auto-test features, which automatically perform a series of tests on the cable.
- **Network monitors and protocol analyzers** These tools monitor traffic on the network and display the packets that have been transmitted across the network.
- **Crossover cable** This tool is a twisted-pair cable with two wires crossed that is used to connect two computers to each other directly without the use of a hub. A crossover cable is also used to connect hubs together in the event you need to cascade them.
- **Hardware loopback adapter** This tool helps to test the ports on a system without having to connect to an external device. One example is a serial loopback adapter.

SIMPLEX, HALF-DUPLEX, AND FULL DUPLEX

When data travels across the medium, it travels in a certain direction. To describe the movement of data across communication channels, certain terms are used, including the following:

- **Simplex** It refers to data moving in a single direction.
- **Half-duplex** It means data travels in both ways, but in only one direction at a time.
- **Full duplex** It means data travels simultaneously in both directions.

CABLING

Cabling is a term that can refer to the act of installing the cable and the work performed before installation begins. Because coaxial cable and twisted-pair cable are copper cables, and fiber-optic cable uses glass or plastic fibers, different issues may arise for each type of cable. There are significant differences in how they are created and installed.

Copper Cabling

Installation of cable requires tools which are used to cut and strip the cable and to attach the proper connector to the end of the cable. Some of these tools may include the following:

- **Cable cutter** is a tool which is used to cut the cable to the length you need.
- **Cable stripper** is a tool which is used to strip the cable jacket and expose the copper wire inside.
- **Crimp tool** is a tool which is used to attach the connectors to the cable.
- **Connectors** are tools that are attached at the ends of the cable.

The pulling force of cabling refers to the amount of force or tension that can be placed on the cable without damaging it. The minimum bend radius of a cable refers to how far the cable can be bent before it is damaged.

Fiber Cabling

Fiber cabling also has bend radius and pull force ratings, and during installation, special tools will be needed to strip the cable so that the appropriate connector can be attached. These tools include the following:

- **Cable stripper or ring tool** is a tool which is used to remove the plastic jacket of the cable without damaging the fibers.
- **Kevlar shears** is a tool which is used to cut the kevlar inside the fiber-optic cable.
- **Connectors** are tools that are attached at the ends of the cable.

Preparing Twisted-Pair Cable

Twisted-pair cabling uses color codes to specify the purpose of each wire and to make them easily identifiable. Because each wire belongs to a pair, the colors of each pair are the same, with one solid and the other striped. When connecting

Table 2.3	Twisted-Pair Wire/Pin Placement
Pin	**Wire**
1	Orange and white
2	Orange
3	Green and white
4	Blue
5	Blue and white
6	Green
7	Brown and white
8	Brown

twisted-pair wire to an RJ-45 connector, the wires will have to be aligned so that they match up with the pins of the connector. There are two standards which can be used to place an RJ-45 connector on a twisted-pair cable, T568A and T568B. Table 2.3 shows how the various wires of a four pair cable are installed into the RJ-45 jack according to the T568B standard.

Preparing cable involves multiple steps. Here is an overview of the process.

1. Determine how much cable is needed for a particular run.
2. Use a cable cutter to cut the cable.
3. Strip the sheathing off the cable to expose the copper wires.
4. Untwist the wires within the cable so you can work with them.
5. Trim the leads of all eight wires to a length of, approximately, 0.5 in.
6. Insert the wires into an RJ-45 connector according to the T568A or T568B standard.
7. Insert the connector and the cable into a crimp tool, and with the wires pressed against the end of the connector, squeeze the crimp tool's handle for a few seconds.

Cable Installation

When installing cable you should plan out your approach before beginning. Some things to consider are as follows:

- Determine the location of the hub, switch, router, or patch panel that the cable will connect to.
- Create documentation on where the cables will be installed.
- Test the cables before they're actually installed.
- Ensure that you actually have more than enough cable for the job at hand.
- Mark each end of a cable clearly, using masking tape or some other form of labeling.

- Use cable ties if you need to bundle the cable.
- Determine if plenum-rated cabling is required or not.

CABLE MANAGEMENT

Cable management and termination of cabling runs is important when working in different network topologies. The following are some characteristics and components common to many networks:

- Typically a central concentrator acts as a backbone for the entire switched and routed network.
- Wiring closet where termination devices such as a 66 block or a 110 block and patch panel exist.
  - **66 Block** cross connects that are used primarily for voice connection, although they can be used for data.
  - **110 Block** cross connects that are used primarily with data connections.

EXAM WARNING

Punch down (or impact) tools are handy for working with termination devices. You should know that the cutting blade and shape of the impact tool is different for 66 block connections and 110 block connections. Make sure you use the appropriate tool tip when terminating your cables. You should also test the run and any other cables you are using.

- Distribution systems are the hierarchical system of cross connections that lead to a local private branch exchange, central concentrator, or the central office or elsewhere.

EXAM WARNING

You will use the term cross connect often while working as a technician. For the exam, it's important to remember this term. The term is used as a reference to the cable that runs from one block to another, generally 25-pair cable.

- *Demarc* is a term used to describe where the provider's equipment ends and the private network begins. It is also referred to as the "termination" point of telecommunications from telephone companies inside a facility or building. Demarc extension is a common term used to describe cabling used to connect to a router, switch, or other device from the smart jack.
- The *smart jack* is a term used to describe the box (or case) and internal cards (and other hardware) where you terminate your router or switching device to get access to the lease line company's circuit. For example, you could connect an RJ-45- or RJ-48-based connector into a T1 smart jack and then connect it to your router or channel service unit.

LAN TECHNOLOGIES AND MEDIA STANDARDS

With the development of networking technologies over the years, it became apparent that standards were necessary so components of a network could work together effectively, and successfully transfer data over the network cable. These standards include Ethernet, Fast Ethernet, and Gigabit Ethernet.

Ethernet uses carrier sense multiple access with collision detection (CSMA/CD) for access to the physical medium. The following are the types of Ethernet:

- **Ethernet** It has standard speed of 10 Mbps, coaxial or twisted-pair cable.
- **Fast Ethernet** It has standard speed of 100 Mbps, coaxial or twisted-pair cable.
- **Gigabit Ethernet** It has standard speed of 1 Gbps, twisted-pair or fiber-optic cable.

10Base2, 10Base5, and Arcnet

Various applications of coaxial cabling are as follows:

10Base2:

- 10Base2 is also known as *Thinnet*.
- The cable used in 10Base2 is an RG-58 cable that is 6.3 mm or 0.25 in. in diameter.
- It supports transmission speeds of 10 Mbps.
- It is used on bus topologies, the network cards are attached to the cable using a BNC T-connector, and the backbone cable is terminated at each end using a 50 Ω terminator.
- It has a maximum length of 185 m or 600 ft per segment, and workstations must be spaced a minimum distance of 0.5 m from one another.
- It may use RG-58/U cable which has a solid copper wire.
- It may use RG-58 A/U cable which has a stranded copper wire.
- It may use RG-58 C/U, which is a military implementation of RG-58 A/U.

10Base5:

- 10Base5 is also known as *Thicknet*.
- The cable used in 10Base5 is a coaxial cable that is 13 mm or 0.5 in. in diameter.
- It supports transmission speeds of 10 Mbps.
- It is used on bus topologies, the network cards are attached to the cable using a vampire tap to pierce the cable so that a connection can be made to the cable. An N connector or a cabling tray and a transceiver called a media attachment unit (MAU) are connected to the cable. Another cable called an attachment unit interface (AUI) that can be up to 50 m in length is then run to the network card of the workstation. Each end of the AUI cable uses a 15-pin D-connector, which is also referred to as a Digital-Intel-Xerox (DIX) or DB-15 connector.

- The backbone cable is terminated at each end using a 50 Ω terminator.
- The cable has a maximum length of 500 m or 1640 ft per segment.
- A 10Base5 cable can have no more than 100 taps per cable segment, with each tap spaced 2.5 m apart.
- Determining how long a 10Base5 cable could be lengthened using different segments can be calculated using the 5-4-3 rule. A 10Base5 cable can have up to five segments, with four repeaters, with only three of the segments having devices attached to it.
- A single fault in the cable can bring the entire network down.
- Each end of the cable must be terminated in a bus topology.
- RG-59, which is used for broadband transmissions (such as cable television), is used for 10Base5 networks.
- RG-6, which is used for broadband, supports higher transmission rates than RG-59.
- RG-8 is a 10Base5 cable.

Arcnet:

- Arcnet is a token bus technology.
- It may use RG-62 cable.

10BaseT and Beyond

The various types of media standards for twisted-pair and fiber-optic cabling are shown in Table 2.4.

Table 2.4   Media Standards Using Twisted-Pair and Fiber

Media Standard	Cable Type	Bandwidth	Cable Length
10BaseT	UTP (Category 3 or higher)	10 Mbps	100 m
100BaseTX	UTP (Category 5 or higher)	100 Mbps	100 m
10BaseFL	Fiber optic	10 Mbps	2 km
100BaseFX	Fiber optic	100 Mbps	400 m (half-duplex) or 2 km (full duplex)
1000BaseT	UTP (Category 5 or higher)	1 Gbps (1000 Mbps)	100 m
1000BaseSX	Fiber optic	1 Gbps (1000 Mbps)	550 m (multimode fiber)
1000BaseLX	Fiber optic	1 Gbps (1000 Mbps)	550 m (multimode fiber) or up to 10 km (single mode fiber)
1000BaseCX	Fiber optic	1 Gbps (1000 Mbps)	100 m

CONNECTORS

A *connector* is an interface that provides a connection between a cable and a device. Because the media used on a network can differ, a number of different connectors have been developed over the years.

Twisted-Pair and Coaxial Cable Connectors

Several types of connectors are available for twisted-pair and coaxial cables, which include the following:

- **D connectors** These connectors look like a letter D turned on its side, the number of pins varies.
  - DB9 – It has nine pins.
  - DB15 – It has 15 pins.
  - DB25 – It has 25 pins.
- **RJ connectors**
  - RJ-11 – It is used with twisted-pair by telephone systems and modems. It has four pins.
  - RJ-45 – It is used with twisted-pair for data communications. It has eight pins.
  - RJ-48 – It is the same as RJ-45 connector but is used for STP cable. It has eight pins.
  - RJ-25 – It allows multiple phone lines to be used. It has six pins.
- **DIX connectors** These are a type of D connector, used with AUI connector on 10Base5 cable.
- **BNC connectors** These are threaded connectors used with coaxial cable on 10Base2. BNC-T used to connect a workstation's cable to backbone segment.
- **F-Type connectors** These are used to terminate coaxial cable, commonly on Thinnet and Thicknet.

Fiber Connectors

There are a number of different connectors that are used with fiber-optic cable. As is the case with some of the connectors available for twisted-pair and coaxial cable, some of these are used with older technology and are not routinely seen on modern networks. They include the following:

- **Straight tip** This connector is an older version of connector used on fiber-optic cable and it is often seen on older 10BaseFL networks. It has a screw-on type of locking mechanism that attaches to the tip of a fiber-optic cable and terminates it.
- **Standard connector** This is the most common type of connector used with fiber-optic cable. It terminates the fiber-optic cable by attaching to its end, using a locking mechanism that clicks into place.

- **Local connector** This is a common high-performance connector. The connector is seated into place by pushing it in and snapping it into place.
- **Mechanical transfer registered jack** This is a duplex connector, which uses a form factor and latch that is similar to the RJ-45 connectors. It is easier to terminate and install than some of the other types of fiber-optic connectors.

RECOGNIZING CABLES

There are three types of physical media that can be used on a network: coaxial cable, twisted-pair cable, and fiber-optic cable. These different media types can be further broken down into different categories and types of cabling, which are either used for specific purposes or provide greater bandwidth.

Category 3, 5, 5e, and 6 UTP

The twisted-pair cable for network use contains three or four pairs of wires.

The Electrical Industry Association (EIA) established different categories of UTP. Some of the more common categories are depicted in Table 2.5.

Table 2.5   Categories of Twisted-Pair Cabling

Category	Uses
CAT 3	16 Mbps. Voice communications in newer telephone systems. Rated at 10 MHz, this is the minimum category of UTP that can be used for data transmissions on networks; it can be used for Ethernet, Fast Ethernet, and Token Ring.
CAT 5	100 Mbps (four pairs). Typically used for Ethernet networks running at 10 or 100 Mbps. Used for data and voice transmission; rated at 100 MHz; suitable for Ethernet, Fast Ethernet, Gigabit Ethernet, Token Ring, and 155 Mbps asynchronous transfer mode (ATM).
CAT 5e	1000 Mbps. Recommended for all new installations, and was designed for transmission speeds of up to 1 Gbps (Gigabit Ethernet). Similar to Category 5, but manufacturing process is refined; higher grade cable than Category 5; rated at 200 MHz; and suitable for Ethernet, Fast Ethernet, Gigabit Ethernet, Token Ring, and 155 Mbps ATM.
CAT 6	Same as CAT5e, but higher standard which provides support for 10 Gbps Ethernet. Rated at 250 MHz; suitable for Ethernet, Fast Ethernet, Gigabit Ethernet, Token Ring, and 155 Mbps ATM.

Shielded Twisted Pair

STP has a shield that's usually made of aluminum/polyester that resides between the outer jacket and the wires. The shield is designed to keep more interference out, protecting the wires inside from EMI caused by outside sources. STP also uses a much higher quality protective jacket for greater insulation.

Coaxial Cable

Coaxial (coax) cable has one strand (a solid-core wire) running down the middle of the cable. Around that strand is insulation. Covering that insulation is braided wire and metal foil, which shields against EMI. A final layer of insulation covers the braided wire. The following are the two types of coaxial cabling that may be used to carry data:

- **Thinnet**
  - A flexible cable about 0.25 in. thick.
  - It is used for short-distance communication and is flexible enough to facilitate routing between workstations.
  - It connects directly to a workstation's network adapter card using a BNC T-connector and uses the network adapter card's internal transceiver.
  - 10Base2 refers to Ethernet LANs that use Thinnet cabling.
- **Thicknet**
  - A thicker cable about 0.5 in. thick.
  - It can support data transfer over longer distances than Thinnet.
  - It is usually used as a backbone to connect several smaller Thinnet-based networks.
  - A transceiver is connected directly to Thicknet cable using a connector known as a piercing tap or vampire tap.
  - 10Base5 refers to Ethernet LANs that use Thicknet cabling.

Single Mode and Multimode Fiber-Optic Cable

Optical fibers carry digital data signals in the form of modulated pulses of light. An optical fiber consists of an extremely thin cylinder of glass, called the *core*, surrounded by a concentric layer of glass, known as the *cladding*. A cable may contain either two fibers per cable – one to transmit and one to receive – or a single fiber. The fiber and cladding can be surrounded by a liquid gel that reflects signals back into the fiber to reduce signal loss, or a plastic spacer surrounded by Kevlar fiber. Each of these components making up the fiber-optic cable are further protected by a plastic covering that encases everything within the cable. The following are the two types of fiber-optic cabling that may be used to carry data:

- **Single mode fiber (SMF)** It is designed to transmit a single beam of light from a laser, used for long-distance transmissions.
- **Multimode fiber (MMF)** It is designed to carry multiple beams of light at the same time, using a light-emitting diode (LED) as a light source, used for short distances.

DID YOU KNOW?

There are other technologies that are either new, not readily associated with networking, or often forgotten. Some of these *other media* include the following:

- IEEE1394 is an external bus that supports fast data-transfer rates. Apple Computers originally developed the technology calling it by the proprietary name, FireWire, but it has since been standardized as IEEE1394. It allows a single 1394 port to have up to 63 external devices connected to it.
- Wireless Media transmits data over the air using wireless adapters and wireless routers, so little to no cabling is required for network communication.
- Transceivers (media converters) are the portion of a network interface that transmits and receives electrical signals across the transmission media, as well as being part of the interface that actually connects to the media. Transceiver types can be classified as being either on-board, which are built onto a network card, or external. With external transceivers the media connection is made externally to the NIC using a connector such as an AUI or a DIX that attaches via an extension cable to the NIC.

Summary of Exam Objectives

Cabling and connectors are essential to any network, providing a medium that allows computers to communicate and send data across the network. Cabling can be twisted-pair, coaxial, or fiber optic. Coaxial cabling consists of a single copper wire to carry data, twisted-pair cabling uses pairs of copper wires twisted together, and fiber-optic cabling sends data across the network in the form of modulated pulses of light.

In using the various cables, there are a number of issues that may impact the performance of a network including EMI, RFI, crosstalk, and attenuation. When problems present themselves, tools such as cable testers, tone generators, TDRs, wire map testers, and oscilloscopes may be used to find the cause or location of a problem on the cable.

We also saw that data can travel along a cable in several ways, using a simplex, half-duplex, or full-duplex data transfer, and that Ethernet is a standard that's used on most networks today. Ethernet has specifications for 10Base2, 10Base5, and 10BaseT networks, and it uses CSMA/CD for collision detection.

10Base2 and 10Base5 are networks that use coaxial cable to transfer data, while 10BaseT, 100BaseTX, and 1000BaseT use UTP or STP cabling, and 10BaseFL, 100BaseFX, 100BaseSX, 1000BaseLX, and 1000BaseCX are based on fiber.

Top Five Toughest Questions

1. You are the network administrator of a 10BaseT network. On the weekend, when few people are working, you run 110 m of cable to a new server that is being used as a file server. The cable is installed in a new section of the building, where no cabling currently exists. When you attempt to access files on the server, they are experiencing errors and corrupt data. Which of the following is most likely the cause of this problem?
   A. Bandwidth
   B. Attenuation
   C. Crosstalk from a neighboring cable
   D. CSMA/CD issues

2. Your company uses UTP cable for all of its network connections including workstations and servers. The users have reported problems connecting to one of the most important servers on the network, and you have been called in to look at it due to a possible physical security breach by a former employee. While examining the server, you find that a small battery-powered motor has been placed and is running next to the server's network connection. What is causing the network problem?
   A. Electromagnetic interference
   B. Static electricity
   C. Transceivers
   D. Unknown, but the motor is probably unrelated

3. You have been hired by a small company to cable its network. The company has offices in two buildings that are 300 m apart. Both of the offices have about 15 computers and the numbers are expected to grow in near future. All of the computers are within 90 m of one another. You need to decide on the cabling that will be used both in the individual buildings and which will be used to connect the buildings LANs together. Which of the following will you do?
   A. Use UTP cabling in each of the buildings, and connect the two buildings together using 10BaseT cabling

B. Use fiber-optic cabling in each of the buildings, and connect the two buildings together using 10Base2 cabling

C. Use 10BaseT cabling in each of the buildings, and connect the two buildings together using 10Base5 cabling

D. Use 100BaseFX cabling in each of the buildings, and connect the two buildings together using 10BaseT cabling

4. Your network uses 100BaseFX so that data can be transferred at higher speeds and up to distances of 400 m. During transmission, data can travel in both directions, but only in one direction at a given time. Which of the following transmission methods is used?

A. Simplex

B. FireWire

C. Half-duplex

D. Full duplex

5. You are the network engineer assigned to implement a new 100 Mbps network connection. You need to select the correct cabling, as well as the correct standard. From the selections below; choose which 100 Mbps networking standard makes use of only two pairs of a Category 5 UTP cable.

A. 10BaseT

B. 100BaseFL

C. 100BaseTX

D. 100BroadT4

Answers

1. Correct answer and explanation: **B.** Attenuation occurs when data transmitted over media weakens over distance. The scenario states that the cable length is 110 m, which is 10 m longer than the maximum distance for 10BaseT.

   Incorrect answers and explanations: **A**, **C**, and **D**. Answer **A** is incorrect because bandwidth is a measurement of the amount of data that can be passed over a cable in a given amount of time. Answer **C** is incorrect because the cable is being installed in a section of the building where no other cabling currently exists. Crosstalk occurs when the electromagnetic field of one wire interferes with the transmission of another. Answer **D** is incorrect because Carrier Sense Multiple Access with Collision Detection (CSMA/CD) prevents devices from interfering with one another during transmission by detecting collisions of data. It is not a cause for data to weaken or be corrupt.

2. Correct answer and explanation: **A.** Electromagnetic interference (EMI) is a low voltage, low current, high frequency signal that can interfere with the electronic signals transmitted over cabling. The motor is powered by

electromagnets whose presence can interfere with the flow of electrons along the UTP cable.

Incorrect answers and explanations: **B, C,** and **D.** Answer **B** is incorrect because static electricity may cause damage to network cards and other electronics, but will not interfere with network traffic on a UTP cable. Answer **C** is incorrect because transceivers are the portion of a network interface that transmits and receives electrical signals across the transmission media. It is unlikely that this is a cause of the problem. Answer **D** is incorrect because the small motor is most likely to be the source of this interference. Anytime a UTP cable is near EMI there will be communications problems.

3. Correct answer and explanation: **C.** Use 10BaseT cabling in each of the buildings, and connect the two buildings together using 10Base5 cabling. The two offices can be connected using thick coaxial cable (10Base5), which can transfer data up to 500 m. 10BaseT can be used within the buildings because it supports distances of 100 m.

   Incorrect answers and explanations: **A, B,** and **D.** Answer **A** is incorrect because 10BaseT has a distance limitation of 100 m. This means that the two buildings can't be connected together. Answer **B** is incorrect because 10Base2 has a distance limitation of 185 m, which is too short for the two buildings. Answer **D** is also incorrect because 10BaseT has a distance limitation of 100 m.

4. Correct answer and explanation: **C.** Half-duplex. 100BaseFX is an Ethernet standard that uses fiber-optic cabling. It can transmit data at speeds of 100 Mbps, but if communication is half-duplex, it can transmit data across cable segments that are up to 400 m in length. If full duplex is used, then it can transmit data up to 2 km. Because data travels both ways on the medium but in only one direction at a time, half-duplex is being described.

   Incorrect answers and explanations: **A, B,** and **D.** Answer **A** is incorrect because simplex refers to data moving in a single direction. Answer **B** is incorrect because FireWire is a proprietary name for IEEE1394, which is an external bus that supports fast data-transfer rates of 400 Mbps and 800 Mbps. Answer **D** is incorrect because full duplex refers to data traveling in both directions simultaneously.

5. Correct answer and explanation: **C.** 100BaseTX uses two UTP pairs (four wires) in a Category 5 UTP cable.

   Incorrect answers and explanation: **A, B,** and **D.** Answer **A** is incorrect because 10BaseT requires Category 3 UTP and only operates at 10 Mbps. Answer **B** is incorrect because 100BaseFL doesn't exist, it's really 10BaseFL, and it requires 10 Mbps fiber-optic cable. Answer **D** is incorrect because 100BoardT4 is not a legitimate networking standard.

CHAPTER 3
Network Devices

NETWORK DEVICES

Network devices are the components of a set of interconnected computer systems that understand the network layout and can efficiently route traffic to its intended destination. They generally connect to each of the computer systems in the network via the types of physical media covered in Chapter 2 and provide security features in addition to the features centered on establishing and maintaining efficient connectivity.

Fast Facts

There exist a number of different network devices, including routers, switches, and hubs, each of which maps to a particular layer of the Open Systems Interconnection (OSI) model. Table 3.1 displays some of these devices and their mappings.

Repeaters

The repeater will take a signal that may be weakening and regenerate it to its original strength so that the data doesn't corrupt as it travels over long distances.

Hubs

Hubs, or concentrators, are central devices where network cabling is connected. Multiple cables connect into the hub, providing a method for data to be passed from one cable to another. Characteristics of a hub are as follows:

Table 3.1	Mapping of Network Devices to the OSI Model
OSI Layer	**Devices**
Application	Application proxy, gateway
Presentation	Gateway
Session	Gateway
Transport	Gateway
Network	Router, multilayer or Layer 3 switches, gateway
Data Link	Network interface card, bridge, Layer 2 switches, access point, gateway
Physical	Hub, multistation access unit, repeater, gateway

- A star topology uses a hub to connect workstations, servers, and other devices.
- A hub takes data and passes it to all ports, allowing the data to travel along the other cables to workstations and devices that are attached to it.
- Hubs have multiple ports and can be uplinked together to provide additional connectivity.
- The 5-4-3 rule applies. It states that you can only connect a total of 5 segments linked together via 4 hubs and only 3 of those segments can be populated with network hosts such as PCs or printers. Breaking rules of this kind could lead to a degradation of performance and possible problems.

There are two main types of hubs:

- **Passive** Passive hubs receive data from one port of the hub and send it out to the other ports. A passive hub contains no power source or electrical components.
- **Active** Active hubs (multiport repeaters) provide the same functionality that a passive hub does, with the additional capability to repeat or regenerate the data.

EXAM WARNING

Hubs operate at the physical layer, Layer 1, of the OSI model. Hubs are designed to forward data from one port of the hub to another, so they don't use upper-layer protocols like Internet Protocol (IP), Internetwork Packet Exchange (IPX), or Media Access Control (MAC) addressing to ensure data reaches its intended destination.

Bridges

Bridges have the capability to forward packets of data based on MAC addresses. A bridge can look at a packet of data and determine the source and destination involved in the transfer of packets. It will read the specific physical address of a packet on one network segment and then decide to filter out the packet or forward it to another segment. A bridge is a simple way to accomplish network segmentation. Bridges segment the network by MAC addresses.

> **EXAM WARNING**
>
> Bridges operate at the data link layer, Layer 2, of the OSI model and use physical addressing to join several networks into a single network efficiently.

Multistation Access Units

Multistation access units (also known as MAUs or MSAUs) are used to connect workstations on a Token Ring network. A MAU typically has eight or more ports that provide connections for workstations and other network devices on a Token Ring network.

Crunch Time

Convergence occurs when vendors put many features into one device. As time goes on, you can expect to see other devices converging together, requiring networks to have fewer components. When you are taking the Network+ exam, it is wise to consider such devices as separate, rather than as one device providing all features. For example, even though your router for the Internet has a firewall, you should consider a router and a firewall as two separate components of a network when taking the exam.

Understanding Switches

A switch stores Layer 2 address information (MAC addresses) regarding each host connected to it. When a frame sent from a host attached to the switch enters the switch port, the switch reads through the MAC address information to determine which port the destination host is attached to and then sends the frame out that port. The only time a switch will send out the data to all of its ports is when a broadcast message is sent.

Broadcast messages are messages that are sent out to all the nodes in a broadcast domain. While the basic functionality of a switch is similar to a hub, there are some fundamental differences. Switches offer full-duplex dedicated bandwidth to local area network (LAN) segments or desktops. You can think of a switch as an intelligent hub that guarantees a specific amount (10, 100, or 1000 Mbps) of bandwidth to the computer that it is connected to. With a hub, you are guaranteed some of the bandwidth all the time. This means that hubs are not intelligent enough to account for collisions on the network; you may be connected to a 10 Mbps port but you may only be receiving 4 Mbps of throughput because of the amount of traffic on the network. With a switch, you are guaranteed the entire limit of your bandwidth because the switch is intelligent and can examine packets and send them in the right direction.

BASIC SWITCHES

Basic switches look at the MAC address of a packet to determine where it is destined. The MAC address is unique to the network interface card (NIC) and makes it identifiable on the network. When a packet of data is sent to the switch, it includes the MAC address of the destination computer, so the switch can tell which computer the data is meant for. This type of switch is called a Layer 2 switch in that it works at the data link layer of the OSI model.

MULTIPORT BRIDGING

Switches are also sometimes referred to as multiport bridges, as they can perform the same functions as a bridge, which can connect two LANs together or segment a large one into two smaller ones. A switch has multiple ports and thereby has the capability to connect more than two different segments of a network. This allows two different networks to communicate with one another, yet still appear as part of the same network.

NETWORK PERFORMANCE IMPROVEMENT WITH SWITCHING

Switching is a fairly involved process with a relatively simple premise: the most direct path is the fastest. A hub will send from a node to all its ports, a switch only sends it to the port that leads to the proper destination. While a hub gives the data a portion of the bandwidth, the switch gives a guaranteed amount of bandwidth, transmitting the data from the incoming port to the outgoing port to directly reach its intended destination.

MULTILAYER SWITCHES

Multilayer switches use a combination of switching and routing. Because multilayer switches handle routing, they function as both a switch and a router simultaneously. Routing allows a device to determine the best way of sending the data to a destination computer through the use of internal routing tables.

A multilayer switch (also called a Layer 3 switch) works by utilizing switching tables and switching algorithms to determine how to send data via MAC addressing from host to host or device to device.

CONTENT SWITCHES

Content switches use Layers 4 to 7 of the OSI Model, and rather than looking at the individual packets being transmitted, they can use sessions to transmit data between machines. Content switches will also take advantage of caching and load balancing so that the amount of data transmitted across networks and requests processed by a server is reduced.

EXAM WARNING

Switches may operate at more than one layer of the OSI model. They work at the data link layer (Layer 2) and sometimes at the network layer (Layer 3) of the OSI model. Layer 3 switches have an integrated router function that allows them to make decisions as to where the data should be sent.

ADVANCED FEATURES OF A SWITCH

Some switches offer enhanced features that bring improved security, services, and capabilities that were unseen in basic switches that were available in previous years. Some of the advanced features include the following:

- **Power over Ethernet (PoE)** PoE is a technology in which electrical power can be transferred over standard twisted-pair cables to provide power to network devices. PoE allows data and electricity to also be transferred along the same cabling.
- **Spanning Tree Protocol (STP)** STP was developed to prevent broadcast storms that result from looping. It uses an algorithm that identifies that a switch has multiple ways of communicating with a single node. In identifying this, it then determines the best way of communicating with that node and blocks out the other paths.
- **Virtual local area networks (VLANs)** A VLAN is a virtual LAN that is used to allow computers and other network devices to appear as if they are on the same network segment, regardless of where they are physically located.
- **Trunking** Trunking refers to a single network link that allows multiple VLANs to communicate with one another. Two switches can send and receive the network traffic from two or more VLANs using a trunking protocol.
- **Port mirroring** Port mirroring is a process in which all the data sent or received on one port or VLAN is copied to another port and is also known as a *Switched Port Analyzer* (SPAN) or roving analysis port (RAP). This is sometimes used to implement intrusion detection systems (IDSes).
- **Port authentication** Port authentication is a process in which access to a port is given to a device by having that device authenticate itself with a server before communication over the port is allowed.

The Modem and Other Adapters

The modem gets its name from a combination of the terms *modu*lator and *dem*odulator. Modems can be categorized into three types:

- **External modem** is commonly used to provide connectivity between computers, existing as a separate component that is attached to a computer using a cable.

- **Internal modem** performs the same functions as the external modem. The difference is that it is located inside the computer chassis.
- **Multiline rack or shelf-mounted** is a solution that is a single chassis containing a certain number of modem cards that can be connected directly to the network.

ANALOG MODEMS

An analog modem is a communications device that enables a computer to talk to another computer through a standard telephone line. It does this by converting digital data from the computer to analog data for transmission over the telephone line and then back to digital data for the receiving computer. They use an RJ-11 connector.

DIGITAL SUBSCRIBER LINE AND CABLE MODEMS

Cable modems and digital subscriber line (DSL) modems access technology that provides connection speeds in the megabit per second (Mbps) range. Characteristics of cable modems are as follows:

- They use the broadband technology of cable television lines.
- They transmit data into a coaxial-based technology, which is used to split Internet access from television signals.
- The transmission speeds are typically around 1.544 Mbps, but broadband Internet can provide greater speeds allowing a download path of up to 27 Mbps.
- Cable modems communicate with a cable modem termination system (CMTS) and provide a constant connection to the cable service provider that also acts in the role of an Internet service provider (ISP).

Characteristics of DSL modems are as follows:

- They allow simultaneous voice and data communications.
- They transmit and receive data digitally across the phone line's twisted-pair cable providing Internet access using existing telephone wiring.
- They provide transmission speeds of 1.544 Mbps and can go up to data transfer rates of 6.1 Mbps.
- The speed of DSL decreases the further you are from a telephone company's offices or a repeater that regenerates the signal. The closer you are to the telephone company's offices, the faster your DSL connection will be.
- There are several different variations of DSL available (shown in Table 3.2), which offer different data transfer rates and distance limitations.

> **Fast Facts**

An Integrated Services Digital Network (ISDN) is a system of digital telephone connections that enables data to be transmitted simultaneously end to end. It consists of multiple components:

Table 3.2	Types of DSL	
Type of DSL	**Bandwidth**	**Distance Limitations**
Asymmetric digital subscriber line (ADSL)	Downstream: 1.544 to 6.1 Mbps Upstream: 16 to 640 Kbps	Speeds decrease over distance. 1.544 Mbps at 18,000 ft., 2.048 Mbps at 16,000 ft., 6.312 Mbps at 12,000 ft., and 8.448 Mbps at 9,000 ft.
Consumer digital subscriber line (CDSL)	Downstream: 1 Mbps Upstream: Under 1 Mbps	18,000 ft.
DSL Lite or G.Lite	1.544 to 6 Mbps	18,000 ft.
ISDN digital subscriber line (IDSL)	128 Kbps	18,000 ft.
High digital subscriber line (HDSL)	Varies depending on twisted-pair lines. 1.544 Mbps duplex on two twisted-pair lines or 2.048 Mbps duplex on three twisted-pair lines	12,000 ft.
Symmetric digital subscriber line (SDSL)	1.544 Mbps	12,000 ft.
Very high digital subscriber line (VDSL)	Downstream: 12.9 to 52.8 Mbps Upstream: 1.5 to 2.3 Mbps	Speeds decrease over distance. 4,500 ft. at 12.96 Mbps, 3,000 ft. at 25.82 Mbps, and 1,000 ft. at 51.84 Mbps

- **ISDN Channels** An ISDN transmission circuit consists of a logical grouping of data channels which carry voice and data. Each ISDN connection consists of two channels, a B channel and a D channel, each with their own function and bandwidth constraints. The bearer channels (B channels) transfer data and offer a bandwidth of 64 Kbps per each channel, and the data channel (D channel) handles signaling at 16 or 64 Kbps so that the B channel doesn't have to do it. This includes the session setup and teardown using a communications language known as Digital Subscriber Signalling System No. 1 (DSS1). The bandwidth available for the D channel is dependent upon the type of service – *basic rate interfaces* (BRIs) usually require 16 Kbps and *primary rate interfaces* (PRIs) use 64 Kbps. Typically, ISDN service contains two B channels and a single D channel. H channels are used to specify a number of B channels. The following list shows the implementations:
  - **H0** 384 Kbps (six B channels)
  - **H10** 1472 Kbps (23 B channels)
  - **H11** 1536 Kbps (24 B channels)
  - **H12** 1920 Kbps (30 B channels) – Europe

- **ISDN Interfaces** There are two basic types of ISDN service:
  - BRI consists of two 64 Kbps B channels and one 16 Kbps D channel for a total of 144 Kbps. Only 128 Kbps is used for user data transfers. BRIs were designed to enable customers to use their existing wiring. This provided a low-cost solution for customers and is why it is the most basic type of service today intended for small business or home use. To use BRI services, you must subscribe to ISDN services through a local telephone company or provider. By default, you must be within 18,000 ft. (about 3.4 miles) of the telephone company's central office for BRI services.

  - PRI requires T1 carriers to facilitate communications. Normally, the channel structure contains 23 B channels plus one 64 Kbps D channel for a total of 1536 Kbps. This standard is used only in North America and Japan. European countries support a different kind of ISDN standard for PRI. It consists of 30 B channels and one 64 Kbps D channel for a total of 1984 Kbps. A technology known as *Non-Facility Associated Signaling* (NFAS) is available to enable you to support multiple PRI lines with one 64 Kbps D channel.

- **ISDN devices** The standard refers to the devices that are required to connect the end node to the network.

- **ISDN reference points** They are used to define logical interfaces. They are, in effect, a type of protocol used in communications. The following list contains the reference points:
  - **R** defines reference point between a TE2 device and a TA device.

  - **S** defines reference point between TE1 devices and NT1 or NT2 devices.

  - **T** defines reference point between NT1 and NT2 devices.

  - **U** defines reference point between NT1 devices and line termination equipment. This is usually the central switch.

- **ISDN identifiers** They use five separate identifiers when making a connection. The provider assigns two of these when the connection is first set up: the service profile identifier (SPID) and the directory number (DN). These are the most common numbers used because the other three are dynamically set up each time a connection is made. The three dynamic identifiers are terminal endpoint identifier (TEI), bearer code (BC), and service access point identifier (SAPI).

Channel Service Unit/Data Service Unit

Channel service unit/data service unit (CSU/DSU) is a device that takes a signal from a digital medium and multiplexes it. Characteristics of a CSU/DSU include the following:

- It is used to terminate the end of a leased T-carrier line, which is a high-speed line that can be used to connect a LAN to a wide area network (WAN).
- It can be a separate component that attaches to a router and provides an interface.
- Newer routers have more modular capabilities that allow you to purchase what are sometimes referred to as WAN interface cards (WICs) that incorporate the CSU/DSU into the actual port and cable connection.

Network Interface Cards

NICs, also referred to simply as network cards, provide an interface to the network that allows data to be transmitted and received across the network media. Simply put, the NIC performs the following functions:

- It translates data from the parallel data bus to a serial bit stream for transmission across the network.
- It formats packets of data in accordance with protocol.
- It transmits and receives data based on the hardware address of the card.

An NIC works as an interface between a computer's expansion bus and the medium that's used to transmit and receive data across the network.

INSTALLING AN NIC

Installing an NIC is like installing any other interface card in a computer. You have to determine the slot it will go in and have the right tools to remove the expansion slot cover and to remove and insert screws. Newer computers do not require any tools, not even screwdrivers.

NIC TYPES AND OPERATION

There are many different types of media and connectors that may be used on a network, which is why there are different NICs and each NIC has its own corresponding software drivers. Because of this, NICs are often defined by the following criteria:

- The type of Data Link protocol they support, such as an Ethernet or Token Ring
- The type of media they connect to
- The data bus for which they were designed

The NICs that exist in the various workstations on a network communicate with each other using their own unique addresses. The MAC address, or hardware address, is a 12-digit number consisting of digits 0 to 9 and letters A to F. It is a hexadecimal (base16) number assigned to the card by the manufacturer. The MAC address consists of two pieces: the first signifies which vendor it comes from and the second is the serial number unique to that manufacturer. This address must be unique on each network card on a network.

> **EXAM WARNING**
>
> NICs are the most common interface for a computer or device to connect to media on the network. They operate at the data link layer of the OSI model

TRANSCEIVERS

The term *transceiver* is short for transmitter–receiver, and it is a component of an NIC that transmits and receives electrical signals across the transmission media. Transceivers are also the part of the interface that actually connects to the media. While transceivers can be external to the network card, they are typically built onto the NIC. A transceiver that's built onto a card is called an *onboard transceiver*.

Media Converters

Media converters are used when you have two types of dissimilar media that need to be converged. They are most commonly used when deploying fiber networks because there are generally points at which the fiber network will connect to existing copper-based networks. They are primarily used and seen on storage area networks (SAN) since the SAN uses fiber to communicate, but exists within a network that is primarily cabled using copper.

Modern Network Devices

These devices are crucial to a network's capability to handle data and ensure it reaches its intended destination as its being transmitted.

Crunch Time

Routers route data packets across a network by opening the packet and making routing decisions based on the contents. On a network that uses Transmission Control Protocol/Internet Protocol (TCP/IP) as its communication protocol, IP addresses are used as a method of identifying computers. Router characteristics include the following:

- Routers facilitate communications at Layer 3 by addressing messages and translating their logical addresses into an actual physical address.

- Routers separate different broadcast domains from one another and route traffic based on the destination IP address, which is Layer 3 information (the MAC address is at Layer 2).
- Routers use either static or dynamic routing.
  - Static: network administrators manually add, maintain, and delete routes on the network routing devices.
  - Dynamic: routers utilize a routing protocol to dynamically create and remove routes on demand as the network changes.

There are a few situations in which integrating static and dynamic routers is acceptable:

- When you have a router at either end of a slow WAN link, you may wish to use static routes. These routers will not increase traffic by broadcasting updated route information to the router on the other end of the link.
- When you require a packet to travel the same path each time to a remote network, you will need to use static routes. Add the path you would like the packet to take to reach the destination network. You cannot enter the entire path over several routers, only the path to the first router.
- When you want to configure a static router to point toward a dynamic router to take advantage of the dynamic router indirectly. This is the next best thing to using a dynamic router. You can hand off the packet to the dynamic router and let this router determine the most efficient path to the destination based on the paths it has learned from neighboring dynamic routers.

EXAM WARNING

Routers operate at the network layer of the OSI model. The exam will deal with questions regarding both routers and the OSI model.

Switching Routers

Switching routers have the capability to perform the tasks normally associated with other devices. A Layer 3 switch has the capability to open packets and view the IP address and MAC address of the computer the packet is destined for. The switch can then review routing tables on the switch to determine the best route to send the data. By performing these functions, the switch is able to do the work of a router and get the packet to its intended destination by using the best route.

SECURITY INTEGRATION

The need for security in network devices and networks in general continues to grow. Equipment and software can be added to a network, which can work with existing devices to protect your LAN and its data.

DID YOU KNOW?

A firewall protects a secure internal network from a public insecure network. Firewalls have the capability to control the traffic that is sent from an external network, such as the Internet, to an internal network or local computer. Firewalls use advanced techniques to monitor connections, log potential intrusions, and act upon these incidents.

A firewall compares traffic to a set of rules that define how the traffic should be dealt with by the firewall. If the traffic matches the rules for acceptable data, the traffic is passed on to the network. If the rule specifies that the data be denied, the traffic will be discarded. The following are some possible architectural implementations:

- **Dual-homed host firewalls** A dual-homed firewall consists of a single computer with two physical network interfaces. This computer acts as a gateway between two networks.
- **Screened host firewalls** With screened host firewalls, you place a screening router between the gateway host and the public network. This enables you to provide packet filtering before the packets reach the host computer, as depicted in Figure 3.1.
- **Screened subnet firewalls** A screened subnet firewall configuration isolates the internal network from the public network. An additional screening router is placed between the internal network and the firewall proxy server. The internal router handles local traffic while the external router handles inbound and outbound traffic to the public network, as depicted in Figure 3.2.

Firewall Types

There are three basic categories of firewalls:

- **Packet level firewall** This is a form of screening router that examines packets based upon filters that are set up at the network and transport layers. You can block incoming or outgoing transfers based on a TCP/IP address or other rules. Rules can be based on source address, destination address, session protocol type, and the source and destination port. It only functions at Layer 3 rendering this a very basic form of protection.
- **Application level firewall** This firewall understands the data at the application level and functions at the application, presentation, and session layers.
- **Circuit level firewall** This circuit level firewall is similar to an application proxy except that the security mechanisms are applied at the time the connection is established. From then on, the packets flow between the hosts without any further checking from the firewall. Circuit level firewalls operate at the transport layer.

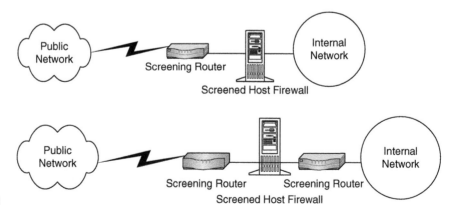

FIGURE 3.1
Screened host firewall

FIGURE 3.2
Screened subnet firewall

Firewall Features

As firewalls have evolved, additional feature sets have been developed for these devices such as:

- Encryption mechanisms.
- Caching for Web services.
- Virtual private network functionality.
- Content filtering from applets, scripts, and components.

Demilitiarized Zone

In computer security, the demilitiarized zone (DMZ) is a neutral network segment where systems accessible to the public Internet are housed, which offers some basic levels of protection against attacks. The creation of these DMZ segments is usually done in one of two ways:

- **Layered DMZ implementation** The systems are placed between two firewall devices with different rule sets, which allows systems on the Internet to connect to the offered services on the DMZ systems, but prevents them from connecting to the computers on the internal segments of the organization's network.
- **Multiple interface firewall implementation** This method involves adding a third interface to the firewall and placing the DMZ systems on that network segment.

The role of the firewall in each of these scenarios is to manage the traffic between the network segments. The basic idea is that other systems on the Internet are allowed to access only the services of the DMZ systems that have been made public. In this way, systems are exposed only to attacks against the services that they offer and not to underlying processes that may be running on them.

Access Control Lists

Access control lists (ACLs) are used to control access to specific resources on a device or network. An ACL resides on a computer or network device and is a table with information on which specific rights have been granted. The operating system or network device uses the ACL to determine whether an allowed or denied privilege is granted.

Proxy Server (Caching Appliances)

A proxy server is a server that performs a function on behalf of another system, typically browser-based requests to and from the Internet. The users perform actions as they normally would but will submit the request to the proxy server. The proxy server will then transmit the request and receive the results often times caching these results for later use.

Proxy servers can:

- Cache information going to/from the Internet.
- Act as the physical gateway between the Internet and company network.
- Be configured with filtering for determining if traffic is to be allowed.

Intrusion Detection System

IDS is designed to inspect and detect the kinds of traffic or network behavior patterns that match known attack signatures or that suggest potential unrecognized attacks may be incipient or in progress.

It is used as a specialized tool that knows how to read and interpret the contents of log files from routers, firewalls, servers, and other network devices. Although such devices tend to operate at network peripheries, IDS systems can detect and deal with insider attacks and external attacks.

OTHER DEVICES AND TECHNOLOGIES

Various devices are used to manage a network and provide additional features that make the network safer and more functional in day-to-day use. Examples of other devices and technologies include the following:

- **Gateways** A gateway is a bridge connecting two dissimilar systems.
- **Default gateways and subnetworks** Default gateways are routers that are used to forward data packets with a destination IP address not on the local subnet. The default gateway forwards the data packet to other gateways until the packet is ultimately delivered to a gateway connected to the intended destination.
- **Wireless** Wireless networks require minimal cabling as data is transmitted over the air using wireless adapters and wireless routers. Computers using wireless NICs use a transceiver that sends and receives signals over the air to a wireless router or hub. The wireless router is an access point providing a method of communication that the computers with wireless NICs can connect to.
- **Network attached storage (NAS)** NAS devices are devices that are dedicated to providing storage of data on the network. NAS uses hard disks for storage, but instead of being installed on a server, the storage device is accessed through its own network address.
- **Domain name service (DNS) Server** DNS is a service that maps IP addresses to names. A HOSTS file can be used to perform the same function, but is a local text file that must be kept up-to-date. DNS provides the same functionality through a centralized database.
- **Dynamic Host Configuration Protocol (DHCP) Server** DHCP is a broadcast-based protocol that is used to automatically assign TCP/IP addressing information to computers. DHCP requires a DHCP Relay server

to service multiple network segments. DHCP can set options such as the network address, subnet mask, gateway, and DNS server address.

- **Voice and IP telephony** Voice over Internet Protocol (VoIP) allows you to talk to people all over the world over the Internet. The phones on the receiving side can be either VoIP or traditional wired phones. You can make local or long distance calls by having them sent as packets across the Internet, thereby avoiding the long distance phone charges that may be associated with the communication.

- **Load balancer** A load balancer is a device that will distribute connection load between multiple devices in your environment that are serving the same function.

- **Multifunction devices** Whether a network printer or server, many devices have the capability to do more than just a single function. You will need to understand how to distinguish the different roles that a single device may play.

Summary of Exam Objectives

There are many devices that make up a network. Hubs are used to provide connectivity by passing from one port in the hub to the others; bridges are used to connect two different LANs or segment a large LAN into two smaller halves. An analog modem is a communications device that enables a computer to talk to another computer through a standard telephone line. Cable modems, which use broadband technology, or DSL, which provides high-speed connections via the twisted-pair cabling of telephone lines, can also be used for connectivity, as can ISDN, which provides 128 Kbps connections over telephone lines. Faster methods of communication can also be acquired using devices like CSU/DSU, which provides an interface to T-carrier lines.

The NIC functions as an interface between computers, printers, and other devices and the physical media on the network by transferring data to the cable. Data on the network may be forwarded to its proper destination using either a switch or a router. A switch takes data from a cable connected to its port, but unlike a hub that forwards the data through all of its other ports, a switch will forward the packet through a single port that leads to the computer that the data is intended for. Switches can also provide the functions of a router, which is used to route data packets across a network by opening the packet and making routing decisions based on the contents.

Network security can be achieved through a variety of devices and concepts. Firewalls are used to secure an internal network from outside influence from a public insecure network. A DMZ can also be used on the network as a neutral network segment where systems accessible to the public Internet are housed, which offers some basic levels of protection against attacks. In addition to this, proxy servers can shield the origins of where data was sent from, as they act on behalf of other systems.

Top Five Toughest Questions

1. You have installed new cabling to accommodate a new section of the building that is being networked. Once computers are installed, you find that they are unable to connect to the network. You believe the problem is that the length of the cabling has exceeded the maximum distance allowed. You want to fix the problem with the least amount of cost and work. Which of the following will you do?

   A. Remove the cabling and install cable that supports a longer distance.

   B. Install a passive hub to increase the distance that data can travel along the cable.

   C. Install an NIC to increase the distance that data can travel along the cable.

   D. Install a switch to increase the distance that data can travel along the cable.

2. What will happen if the default gateway is not specified on your computer and you are trying to reach another network?

   A. The packet will ask every router if they know the path to reach the destination.

   B. The packet will broadcast for the IP address of the nearest router.

   C. The packet will be forwarded to the DNS server.

   D. The packet will not be sent.

3. You have replaced all the hubs in your network with 10/100 Mbps switches. The switch ports are configured to work by automatically sensing the network speed. Most of the workstations already had 10/100 Mbps network adapters. Which of the following will you need to do to upgrade the speed of the entire network to 100 Mbps?

   A. Replace all 10 Mbps network adapters to 10/100 Mbps in the remaining workstations.

   B. Reconfigure all the ports on the switch to operate only at 100 Mbps.

   C. Reconfigure the 10 Mbps adapters in remaining workstations to operate only at 100 Mbps.

   D. None of the above.

4. As a network technician, you are asked to deploy a network load balancer. You need to configure a network load balancer on the 10.0.10.0/8 network for the Web development group. You need to configure it appropriately. From the list of possible deployment scenarios, which would you select from as your design?

   A. You need to distribute the load to a group of Secure Shell (SSH) servers.

   B. You need to centralize your traffic around your File Transfer Protocol (FTP) servers.

   C. You need to distribute the load to a pool of Web servers.

   D. You need to redistribute the traffic to a farm of DHCP servers on your DMZ.

5. You are the administrator of a small business network. You notice that as you add workstations to the network over time the speed of the network decreases; what devices would you replace in your network with what other device to resolve this problem?
  A. Replace repeaters with hubs.
  B. Replace routers with hubs.
  C. Replace routers with switches.
  D. Replace hubs with switches.

Answers

1. Correct answer and explanation: **D.** Install a switch to increase the distance that data can travel along the cable. Switches can perform the same functions that repeaters used to by regenerating the data so that it is sent out from the switch at its original strength.

Incorrect answers and explanations: **A, B,** and **C.** Answer **A** is incorrect because removing the cabling and replacing it with another kind is not only costly, but a considerable amount of work. Answer **B** is incorrect because a passive hub won't regenerate the data when it is sent out from its ports. Answer **C** is incorrect because an NIC is used as an interface to communicate on the network. It isn't used as a means of regenerating data so that the network can be extended.

2. Correct answer and explanation: **D.** The packet will not be sent. Without that default gateway, you are stuck on the local network. The subnet mask, which you will learn about in the next chapter, is also very important. Without a properly configured subnet mask to determine which subnet your computer is on, your computer will be unable to communicate outside the local network.

Incorrect answers and explanations: **A, B,** and **C.** Answer **A** is incorrect because the PC will not know the addresses of the routers to send the data packets to or even inquire about router addresses or destination addresses. Answer **B** is incorrect for the same reason. Answer **C** is incorrect because the DNS server is used for name-to-IP address resolution and not IP addresses of routers.

3. Correct answer and explanation: **A.** Replace all 10 Mbps network adapters to 10/100 Mbps in the remaining workstations. Because the switch ports are configured to automatically sense the network speed, the workstations with 100 Mbps network adapters will communicate with the switch at 100 Mbps and others at 10 Mbps. This will affect the overall network speed. To have a complete 100 Mbps network, you should replace the 10 Mbps adapters with 10/100 Mbps network adapters in the remaining workstations.

Incorrect answers and explanations: **B, C,** and **D.** Answer **B** is incorrect because even if the switch ports are configured to operate at 100 Mbps, the communication with workstations with 10 Mbps adapters will be at 10 Mbps. Answer **C** is incorrect because 10 Mbps adapters cannot be configured to operate at 100 Mbps. Answer **D** is incorrect because answer **A** is a legitimate solution.

4. Correct answer and explanation: **C**. Load balancers are primarily used when working with Web servers. Although load balancers can be used in other situations, you would likely not see them used in the other options and solutions provided for you.

   Incorrect answers and explanations: **A**, **B**, and **D**. Answer **A** is incorrect because you would not use a load balancer in this fashion nor would SSH be used in this way. Answer **B** is incorrect because FTP servers are not in need of load balancing. Answer **D** is incorrect because you would not use a load balancer to balance DHCP requests.

5. Correct answer and explanation: **D**. By replacing hubs with switches, you will reduce the congestion on the network by ensuring that each machine will only need to examine the traffic directed to itself in addition to broadcast traffic. With a hub on the network, all traffic is examined by all computers, causing additional overhead and increasing the number of collisions that occur. By moving to a switch, the collisions are reduced and the traffic is more directed, thus improving performance.

   Incorrect answers and explanations: **A**, **B**, and **C**. Answer **A** is incorrect because a repeater is a device that simply boosts the transmission signal as it travels along the cabling. If there were an inadequate number of connections in the environment, then replacing a repeater with a hub would allow for additional nodes to connect, but would not address the issue of decreased network speed over time. Answer **B** is incorrect because routers and hubs do not serve the same function. Routers isolate broadcast domains and are responsible for routing traffic between segments, while hubs form the segments. Answer **C** is incorrect because routers and switches do not serve the same function. Routers isolate broadcast domains and are responsible for routing traffic between segments, while switches form the segments.

CHAPTER 4

Wireless Networking

Exam objectives in this chapter
- Radio Frequency and Antenna Behaviors and Characteristics
- Wireless Network Concepts
- Common Exploits of Wireless Networks
- Configuring Windows Client Computers for Wireless Network Security
- Site Surveys

RADIO FREQUENCY AND ANTENNA BEHAVIORS AND CHARACTERISTICS

To be well prepared for the exam, you must have a good understanding of basic radio frequency (RF) behaviors and antenna characteristics.

Fast Facts

RF and antenna behaviors play an important part in how wireless networks operate and interact with their environments. They need to be considered as wireless network design decisions are taking place and also can be useful during troubleshooting.

RF behaviors include the following:

- **Gain and loss** Gain occurs when a signal has its strength increased, such as by passing through an amplifier. Loss is the exact opposite of gain, and occurs when a signal has its strength decreased, either intentionally through the use of a device such as an attenuator, or unintentionally such as through reflection and refraction.

- **Reflection and refraction** Reflection occurs when the RF signal impacts a relatively flat and smooth object such as a door, wall, floor, ceiling, or building and the signal is reflected off at a different angle than the entry signal and some signal will be lost due to absorption and scattering. When a wave is refracted, it passes through a medium and changes course with some of the original wave being reflected away from the original wave's path. Refraction is a particular problem for long-range outdoor point-to-point links due to changing atmospheric conditions, notably differing air densities due to changes in air temperature.

- **Diffraction** When a radio wave meets an obstacle, it has a tendency to bend around the obstacle, which is called *diffraction*.

- **Absorption and scattering** Absorption and scattering can absolutely destroy an electromagnetic signal wave and prevent it from reaching its intended destination. Absorption occurs when the RF signal has been completely *absorbed* because it has impacted an object that does not pass it on through any means (reflection or refraction). In this case, no signal is left and the data contained in it is lost. *Scattering* is when an incoming electromagnetic wave hits a surface that is small compared with its wavelength. The resultant effect causes many lower magnitude waves to be sent off at various angles relative to the path of the original wave. Typical sources of scattering include trees, street signs, and atmospheric conditions.

Antenna characteristics include the following:

- **Line of sight and Fresnel zone** With light waves, if a straight line exists, it's implied that the line of sight (LOS) exists. Once you have LOS, the light waves will be able to travel from point to point. This is true for RF as well. However, RF waves are also subject to a phenomenon known as the Fresnel zone (pronounced "fray-nell"), which is an elliptical region extending outward from the visual LOS. When dealing with optics, visual LOS is enough to ensure good signal transmission from point to point, but with electromagnetic waves, objects that extend into the Fresnel zone can cause signal loss through methods such as reflection, refraction, and scattering. Objects including buildings and trees can create a blockage, and to overcome any blockage, you must either remove the object causing the blockage or raise one or both antennas in the link.

WIRELESS NETWORK CONCEPTS

In the past 5 years, two wireless network technologies have seen considerable deployment: wireless application protocol (WAP) networks and wireless local area network (WLAN).

Overview of Wireless Communication in a Wireless Network

Wireless networks rely on the manipulation of an electrical charge to enable communication between devices. A network adapter can decode and encode the electric current to and from meaningful information (bits) that can subsequently be sent or received.

RF COMMUNICATIONS

RF characteristics and facts:

- Wireless networks use a special type of electric current known as RF.
- RF is created by applying alternating current (AC) to an antenna to produce an electromagnetic (EM) field.
- Wireless networks use the *EM field* for communications, which is the region of space that is influenced by EM radiation.
- On wireless networks, amplitude decreases with distance, resulting in the degradation of signal strength and the ability to communicate.
- Radio waves are affected by the presence of obstructions and can be reflected, refracted, diffracted, or scattered, depending on the properties of the obstruction and its interaction with the radio waves, all of which result in signal degradation.
- The interference created by bounced radio waves is called *multipath interference*. Common sources of multipath interference include metal doors, metal roofs, water, metal vertical blinds, and any other source that is highly reflective to radio waves.
- EM fields are also prone to interference and signal degradation by the presence of other EM fields, such as interference produced by cordless phones, microwave ovens, and a wide range of devices that use the same bands.
- To mitigate the effects of interference from these devices and other sources of electromagnetic interference, RF-based wireless networks employ spread spectrum technologies. Wireless networks use a "spectrum" of frequencies for communication.

SPREAD SPECTRUM TECHNOLOGY

Spread spectrum technology characteristics and facts:

- Spread spectrum defines methods for wireless devices to send a number of narrowband frequencies over a range of frequencies simultaneously for communication.
- The narrowband frequencies used between devices change according to a random-appearing, but defined pattern, allowing individual frequencies to contain parts of the transmission.

Crunch Time

Two methods of synchronizing wireless devices are as follows:

- **Frequency hopping spread spectrum (FHSS)** FHSS works by quickly moving from one frequency to another, according to a pseudorandom pattern. The frequency range used by the frequency hop is relatively large (83.5 MHz), providing excellent protection from interference. The amount of time spent on any given frequency is known as *dwell time*, and the amount of time it takes to move from one frequency to another is known as *hop time*. Wireless networks that use FHSS include *HomeRF* and *Bluetooth*.

- **Direct sequence spread spectrum (DSSS)** DSSS works by dividing the data and simultaneously transmitting on as many frequencies as possible within a particular frequency band (also known as a *channel*). DSSS adds redundant bits of data known as *chips* to the data to represent binary 0s or 1s. The ratio of chips-to-data is known as the *spreading ratio*: the higher the ratio, the more immune to interference the signal is, because if part of the transmission is corrupted, the data can still be recovered from the remaining part of the chipping code. Additionally, DSSS protects against data loss through the redundant, simultaneous transmission of data.

WIRELESS NETWORK ARCHITECTURE

Wireless networks operate at the physical and data link layers of the open system interconnection (OSI) model. Both FHSS and DSSS are implemented at the physical layer of the OSI model. The data link layer is divided into two sublayers: the media access control (MAC) and logical link control (LLC) layers.

The MAC layer is responsible for such things as framing data, error control, synchronization, and collision detection and avoidance. Wireless networks utilize carrier sense multiple access with collision avoidance (CSMA/CA) method for protecting against data loss. Using CSMA/CA, a wireless workstation first tries to detect if any other device is communicating on the network. If it senses it is clear to send, it initiates communication.

Wireless Network Protocols and Operation

WLANs are covered by the IEEE 802.11 standards.

In addition to providing a solution to the problems created by collisions that occur on a wireless network, the 802.11 standard must deal with other issues specific to the nature of wireless devices and wireless communications in general.

WIRELESS APPLICATION PROTOCOL

- An open specification designed to enable mobile wireless users to easily access and interact with information and services.
- WAP is designed for hand-held digital wireless devices.
- WAP browsers in a wireless client are analogous to the standard Internet browsers on computers.
- WAP uniform resource locators (URLs) are the same as those defined for traditional networks and are also used to identify local resources in the WAP-enabled client.
- The WAP specification added two significant enhancements to the above programming model: push and telephony support (wireless telephony application [WTA]).
- WAP also provides for the use of proxy servers, as well as supporting servers that provide functions such as public key infrastructure support, user profile support, and provisioning support.

WIRELESS TRANSPORT LAYER SECURITY

- Wireless transport layer security (WTLS) is an attempt to introduce security into WAP.
- The WTLS protocol is based on the transport layer security (TLS) protocol.
- WTLS is designed to provide privacy as well as reliability for both the client and the server over an unsecured network and is specific to applications that utilize WAP.

DID YOU KNOW?

The original *IEEE 802.11 standard* defines the operation of wireless networks operating in the 2.4 GHz range, using either DSSS or FHSS at the physical layer of the OSI model. This standard also defines the use of infrared for wireless communication. Because of the need for higher rates of data transmission and to provide more functionality at the MAC layer, the 802.11 Task Group developed other standards.

Additional 802.11 standards are listed in Table 4.1

Table 4.1	Additional 802.11 Standards
802.11 Standard	**Details**
IEEE 802.11b	Defines DSSS networks that use the 2.4 GHz industrial, scientific, and medical (ISM) band.
	Supports data transmission at speeds of 1, 2, 5.5, and 11 Mbps.
	Defines the operation of only DSSS devices and is backward compatible with 802.11 DSSS devices.
	Frame type has a maximum length of 2346 bytes.
	Regarding wired equivalent privacy (WEP), the standard defines the use of only 64-bit encryption. The effective key length is only actually 40 bits as there is a 24-bit initialization vector (IV). This leads people and literature to sometimes refer to WEP as 40-bit encryption adding to confusion in discussions.
IEEE 802.11a	A more recent standard than 802.11b.
	Defines networks that use the 5 GHz Unlicensed National Information.
	Infrastructure (U-NII) bands.
	Supports data transmissions of 6, 9, 12, 16, 18, 24, 36, 48, and 54 Mbps.
	Does not use spread spectrum and quadrature phase shift keying (QPSK) as a modulation technique at the physical layer.

(Continued)

Table 4.1 (Continued)	
802.11 Standard	**Details**
	Uses a modulation technique known as orthogonal frequency division multiplexing (OFDM).
	To be 802.11a compliant, devices are only required to support data rates of 6, 12, and 24 Mbps – the standard does not require the use of other data rates.
	802.11a is not backward compatible with 802.11 b because of the use of a different frequency band and the use of OFDM at the physical layer.
	802.11a and 802.11b devices can be easily colocated because their frequencies will not interfere with each other.
IEEE 802.11g	Defines networks that use the ISM 2.4 GHz bands.
	Supports data transmission rates up to 54 Mbps.
	Backward compatibility with 802.11b.
	To achieve the higher rates of transmission, 802.11g devices use OFDM in contrast to QPSK, which is used by 802.11b devices as a modulation technique.
	802.11g devices are able to automatically switch to QPSK to communicate with 802.11b devices.
IEEE 802.11n	To provide both higher data rates (up to 300 Mbps) in the ISM 2.4 GHz bands and the 5 GHz U-NII band, 802.11n was introduced.
	It is backward compatible with 802.11b/g.
	To achieve the higher rates of transmission, 802.11n devices use multiple input/multiple output (MIMO) to take advantage of multiple antennas.

EXAM WARNING

You need to be familiar with the 802.11 standards, the speeds, operation, and so on, for the Network+ exam.

Ad Hoc and Infrastructure Network Configuration

The 802.11 standard provides for two modes for wireless clients to communicate: ad hoc and infrastructure. The ad-hoc mode is geared for a network of stations within communication range of each other and is created spontaneously between the network participants. In infrastructure mode, access points (APs) provide more permanent structure for the network. An infrastructure consists of one or more APs as well as a wired network behind the APs that tie the wireless network to the rest of the network infrastructure.

To distinguish different wireless networks from one another, the 802.11 standard defines the Service Set Identifier (SSID), which is considered the identity element that "glues" various components of a WLAN together. Traffic from wireless clients that use one SSID can be distinguished from other wireless traffic using a different SSID. 802.11 traffic can be subdivided into three parts, which are as follows:

- **Control frames** include such information as request to send (RTS), clear to send (CTS), and acknowledgement (ACK) messages.
- **Management frames** include beacon frames, probe request/response, authentication frames, and association frames.
- **Data frames** 802.11 frames that carry data, which is typically considered network traffic, such as Internet Protocol (IP)-encapsulated frames.

IEEE 802.15 (BLUETOOTH)

Bluetooth uses the same 2.4 GHz frequency that the IEEE 802.11b and 802.11g wireless networks use. Bluetooth characteristics are as follows:

- Bluetooth can select from up to 79 different frequencies within a radio band.
- Bluetooth networks allow clients to be connected to seven networks at the same time.
- Bluetooth devices typically have a maximum useable range of about 10 m (33 ft.).
- Bluetooth is not intended for the long ranges or high data throughput rates.

INFRARED

Infrared is not a standard itself, but rather is the focus of the Infrared Data Association (IrDA). The IrDA's primary function is to create and promote a standardized data-transmission mechanism using infrared light. Infrared characteristics are as follows:

- Infrared devices typically can achieve a maximum data throughput of 4 Mbps.
- Infrared is susceptible to light-based interference.
- Infrared does not interfere in any way with RF-based wireless technologies.
- There is some inherent security in infrared technology due to the fact that an attacker would have to be in the direct path of the transmission.

WIRED EQUIVALENT PRIVACY

RF poses challenges to privacy in that it travels through and around physical objects. Because of the nature of the 802.11 wireless LANs, the Institute of Electrical and Electronics Engineers (IEEE) working group implemented a mechanism to protect the privacy of the individual transmissions, known as the wired equivalent privacy (WEP) protocol.

WEP characteristics:

- WEP utilizes a shared-key authentication that allows for encryption and decryption of wireless transmissions.
- Up to four keys can be defined on an AP or a client, and they can be rotated to add complexity for a higher security standard in the WLAN policy.
- The driving force behind WEP was privacy. In cases that require high degrees of security, other mechanisms should be utilized such as authentication, access control, password protection, and virtual private networks (VPNs).
- Despite its flaws, WEP still offers a better level of security than open wireless connections.

EXAM WARNING

Most APs advertise that they support WEP in 64-bit encryption, but often the 128-bit option is also supported. For corporate networks, 128-bit encryption-capable devices should be considered as a minimum.

With data security enabled in a closed network, the settings on the client for the SSID and the encryption keys must match the AP when attempting to associate with the network or it will fail. WEP provides security and privacy in transmissions held between the AP and the clients. Some of the other benefits of implementing WEP include the following:

- All messages are encrypted using a CRC-32 checksum to provide some degree of integrity.
- Privacy is maintained through the RC4 encryption. Without possession of the secret key, the message cannot be decrypted.
- WEP is extremely easy to implement. All that is required is to set the encryption key on the APs and on each client.
- WEP provides a basic level of security for WLAN applications.
- WEP keys are user-definable and unlimited. WEP keys can, and should, be changed often.

EXAM WARNING

Do not confuse WAP and WEP. Although it may seem that WEP is the privacy system for WAP, you should remember that WTLS is the privacy mechanism for WAP and WEP is the privacy mechanism for 802.11 WLANs.

WPA AND WPA2

Because of the relative ease that WEP with a preshared key can be broken, the Wi-Fi Alliance has created a new encryption standard called Wi-Fi protected access (WPA). WPA enhances security over WEP by using the Temporal Key Integrity Protocol (TKIP) to address some of the weaknesses of WEP including per-packet mixing, a message integrity check, an extended initialization vector (IV), and dynamic rekeying.

Creating Privacy with WEP

WEP provides for three implementations: no encryption, 64-bit encryption, and 128-bit encryption. No encryption means *no privacy*. In 64-bit and 128-bit varieties, the greater the number of characters (bits), the stronger the encryption. The initial configuration of the AP includes the setup of the shared key, which can be in the form of either alphanumeric or hexadecimal strings, and must be matched on the client.

WEP uses the RC4 encryption algorithm, a *stream cipher*, where both the sender and the receiver use the stream cipher to create identical pseudorandom strings from a known shared key. The receiver takes the shared key and identical stream and reverses the process to gain the plaintext transmission.

The steps in the process are as follows:

1. The plaintext message is run through an integrity check algorithm (the 802.11 standard specifies the use of CRC-32) to produce an integrity check value (ICV).
2. This value is appended to the end of the original plaintext message.
3. A "random" 24-bit IV is generated and prepended to (added to the beginning of) the secret key (which is distributed through an out-of-band method) that is then input to the RC4 Key Scheduling Algorithm (KSA) to generate a seed value for the WEP pseudorandom number generator (PRNG).
4. The WEP PRNG outputs the encrypting cipher-stream.
5. This cipher-stream is then XOR'd with the plaintext/ICV message to produce the WEP ciphertext.
6. The ciphertext is then prepended with the IV (in plaintext), encapsulated, and transmitted. A new IV is used for each frame to prevent the reuse of the key from weakening the encryption. WEP incorporates a checksum into each frame. Any frame not found to be valid through the checksum is discarded.

AUTHENTICATION

There are two authentication methods in the 802.11 standard: open and shared-key. Open authentication is more precisely described as device-oriented authentication and can be considered a null authentication – all requests are granted. Without WEP, open authentication leaves the WLAN wide open to any client who knows the SSID. With WEP enabled, the WEP secret key becomes the indirect authenticator.

EXAM WARNING

Open authentication can also require the use of a WEP key. Do not assume that just because the Network+ exam discusses open authentication that a WEP key should not be set.

The shared-key authentication process is a four-step process that begins when the AP receives the validated request for association. The four steps break down in the following manner:

1. The requestor (the client) sends a request for association.
2. The authenticator (the AP) receives the request, and responds by producing a random challenge text and transmitting it back to the requestor.
3. The requestor receives the transmission, encrypts the challenge with the secret key, and transmits the encrypted challenge back to the authenticator.
4. The authenticator decrypts the challenge text and compares the values against the original. If they match, the requestor is authenticated. However, if the requestor does not have the shared key, the cipher stream cannot be reproduced, therefore the plaintext cannot be discovered, and theoretically the transmission is secured.

One of the greatest weaknesses in shared-key authentication is that it provides an attacker with enough information to try to crack the WEP secret key. The challenge, which is sent from authenticator to requestor, is sent in the clear. The requesting client then transmits the same challenge, encrypted using the WEP secret key, back to the authenticator. An attacker who captures both of these packets now has two pieces of a three-piece puzzle: the clear text challenge and the encrypted cipher text of that challenge. The algorithm RC4 is also known. All that is missing is the secret key. To determine the key, the attacker may simply try a brute force search of the potential key space using a dictionary attack. In cryptography, this attack is termed a *known-plaintext* attack and is the primary reason why shared-key authentication is actually considered slightly weaker than open authentication.

802.11I AUTHENTICATION

The IEEE 802.11i standard was created for the purpose of providing a security framework for port-based access control that resides in the upper layers of the protocol stack. The most common method for port-based access control is to enable new authentication and key management methods without changing current network devices. The benefits that are the end result of this work include the following:

1. There is a significant decrease in hardware cost and complexity.
2. There are more options, allowing administrators to pick and choose their security solutions.
3. The latest and greatest security technology can be installed and should still work with the existing infrastructure.
4. You can respond quickly to security issues as they arise.

When a client device connects to a port on an 802.11i-capable AP, the AP port determines the authenticity of the devices. Before we discuss the workings of the 802.11i standard, the following terminology must be defined:

- **Port** A single point of connection to a network.
- **Port access entity (PAE)** Controls the algorithms and protocols that are associated with the authentication mechanisms for a port.
- **Authenticator PAE** Enforces authentication before allowing access to resources located off of that port.
- **Supplicant PAE** Tries to access the services that are allowed by the authenticator.
- **Authentication server** Used to verify the supplicant PAE. It decides whether or not the supplicant is authorized to access the authenticator.
- **Extensible Authentication Protocol Over LAN (EAPoL)** 802.11i defines a standard for encapsulating EAP messages so that they can be handled directly by a LAN MAC service. 802.11i tries to make authentication more encompassing, rather than enforcing specific mechanisms on the devices. Because of this, 802.111i uses Extensible Authentication Protocol (EAP) to receive authentication information.
- **Extensible Authentication Protocol Over Wireless (EAPoW)** When EAPoL messages are encapsulated over 802.11 wireless frames, they are known as *EAPoW*.

The 802.11i standard works in a similar fashion for both EAPoL and EAPoW. The EAP supplicant (in this case, the wireless client) communicates with the AP over an "uncontrolled port." The AP sends an EAP request/identity to the supplicant and a remote authentication dial-in user service (RADIUS)-access-request to the RADIUS access server. The supplicant then responds with an identity packet and the RADIUS server sends a challenge based on the identity packets sent from the supplicant. The supplicant provides its credentials in the EAP-response that the AP forwards to the RADIUS server. If the response is valid and the credentials validated, the RADIUS server sends a RADIUS-access-accept to the AP, which then allows the supplicant to communicate over a "controlled" port. This is communicated by the AP to the supplicant in the EAP-success packet.

User Identification and Strong Authentication

With the addition of the 802.1x standard, clients are identified by username, not by the MAC addresses of the devices. This design not only enhances security, but also streamlines the process of authentication, authorization, and accountability (AAA) for the network. 802.1x was designed to support extended forms of authentication using password methods (such as one-time passwords, or GSS_API mechanisms like Kerberos) and nonpassword methods (such as biometrics, Internet key exchange [IKE], and smart cards).

Dynamic Key Derivation

The IEEE 802.1x standard allows for the creation of per-user session keys. WEP keys do not have to be kept at the client device or at the AP when using 802.1x. These WEP keys are dynamically created at the client for every session, thus making it more secure. The global key, like a broadcast WEP key, can be encrypted using a unicast session key, and then sent from the AP to the client in a much more secure manner.

Mutual Authentication

802.1*x* and EAP provide for a mutual authentication capability. This makes the clients and the authentication servers mutually authenticating end points, and assists in the mitigation of attacks from man-in-the-middle (MITM) types of devices. Any of the following EAP methods provide for mutual authentication:

- **TLS** requires that the server supply a certificate and establish that it has possession of the private key.
- **IKE** requires that the server show possession of a preshared key or private key (this can be considered certificate authentication).
- **GSS_API (Kerberos)** requires that the server can demonstrate knowledge of the session key.

Per-Packet Authentication

EAP can support per-packet authentication and integrity protection, but it is not extended to all types of EAP messages. For example, negative acknowledgment (NACK) and notification messages cannot use per-packet authentication and integrity. Per-packet authentication and integrity protection works for the following (packet is encrypted unless otherwise noted):

- TLS and IKE derive session key
- TLS cipher suite negotiations (not encrypted)
- IKE cipher suite negotiations
- Kerberos tickets
- Success and failure messages that use a derived session key (through WEP)

COMMON EXPLOITS OF WIRELESS NETWORKS

In general, attacks on wireless networks fall into four basic categories: passive, active, MITM, and jamming.

Passive Attacks on Wireless Networks

A passive attack occurs when someone listens to or eavesdrops on network traffic. Passive attacks on wireless networks are extremely common, almost to the point of being ubiquitous. Detecting and reporting on wireless networks has become a popular hobby for many wireless war-driving enthusiasts.

- **Detecting wireless networks** Utilizing new tools created for wireless networks and the existing identification and attack techniques and utilities originally designed for wired networks, attackers have many avenues into a wireless network. The first step in attacking a wireless network involves finding a network to attack. The most popular software developed to identify wireless networks is the Windows-based NetStumbler (www.netstumbler.com). This type of scan, driving around looking for wireless networks, is known as *war driving*.

- **Protecting against wireless network detection** To defend against the use of NetStumbler and other programs to detect a wireless network easily, administrators should configure the wireless network as a closed system. This means that the AP will not respond to empty set SSID beacons and will consequently be "invisible" to programs such as NetStumbler, which rely on this technique to discover wireless networks.

Crunch Time

Sniffing

Sniffing is the electronic form of eavesdropping on the communications that computers transmit across networks. Wireless networks function very similarly to the original repeaters and hubs by allowing every communication across the wireless network to be viewable to anyone who happens to be listening to the network. In fact, the person who is listening does not even need to be associated with the network in order to sniff!

The hacker has many tools available to attack and monitor a wireless network. These tools work well for sniffing both wired and wireless networks. All of these software packages function by putting your network card in what is called *promiscuous mode*. When the network interface controller is in this mode, every packet that goes past the interface is captured and displayed within the application window.

- **Protecting against sniffing and eavesdropping** To protect wireless users from attackers who might be sniffing is to utilize encrypted sessions wherever possible: SSL for e-mail connections, secure shell (SSH) instead of Telnet, and secure copy (SCP) instead of file transfer protocol (FTP). Additionally turn off any network identification broadcasts and, if possible, close down the network to any unauthorized users.

Active Attacks on Wireless Networks

The mechanisms used in active attacks can be comprised of a combination of methods that ultimately result in an intruder being able to navigate his or her way through the interworking of your network. Some possible attack methods include the following:

- **Spoofing and network hijacking** Usage of a legitimate IP address or MAC address by an unauthorized device oftentimes resulting in the redirection of legitimate data packets to the unauthorized device.
- **MITM through rogue APs** Interception of network communications through deployment of an AP with enough strength so that the end users may not be able to tell which AP is the authorized one that they should be using. Using this technique, the attacker is able to receive authentication requests and information from the end workstation regarding the secret key and where they are attempting to connect.

- **Denial of service (DoS) and flooding attacks** A DoS occurs when an attacker has engaged most of the resources a host or network has available, rendering it unavailable to legitimate users.

PROTECTION AGAINST SPOOFING AND NETWORK HIJACKING

Protecting against these attacks involves adding several additional components to the wireless network. The following are examples of measures that can be taken:

- Using an external authentication source such as RADIUS or SecurID, will prevent an unauthorized user from accessing the wireless network and the resources with which it connects.
- Requiring wireless users to use a VPN to access the wired network also provides a significant stumbling block to an attacker.
- Allowing only SSH access or SSL-encrypted traffic into the network.
- Many of WEP's weaknesses can be mitigated by isolating the wireless network through a firewall and requiring that wireless clients use a VPN to access the wired network.

There are several different tools that can be used to protect a network from IP spoofing with invalid address resolution protocol (ARP) requests. These tools, such as ArpWatch, notify an administrator when ARP requests are detected, allowing the administrator to take the appropriate action to determine whether someone is attempting to hack into the network.

Another option is to statically define the MAC/IP address definitions. This prevents attackers from being able to IP spoof without having the defined matching pieces of information. The best protection available is to change the secret key on a regular basis and add additional authentication mechanisms such as RADIUS or dynamic firewalls to restrict access to the wired network. However, unless every wireless workstation is secure, an attacker only needs to go after one of the other wireless clients to be able to access the resources available to it.

PROTECTION AGAINST MITM THROUGH ROGUE APS

Regular wireless site surveys can be used to see if someone has violated your company security policy by placing an unauthorized AP on the network, regardless of their intent. Frequent site surveys also have the advantage of uncovering the unauthorized APs that company staff members may have set up in their own work areas, thereby compromising the entire network and completely undoing the hard work that went into securing the network in the first place. This is usually done with no malicious intent, but for the convenience of the user, who may want to be able to connect to the network through his or her laptop in meeting rooms or break rooms or other areas that don't have wired outlets.

PROTECTING AGAINST DOS AND FLOODING ATTACKS

There is little that can be done to protect against DoS attacks. In a wireless environment, an attacker does not have to even be in the same building or neighborhood.

With a good enough antenna, an attacker is able to initiate these attacks from a great distance away.

Using NetStumbler, administrators can identify other networks that may be in conflict. However, NetStumbler will not identify other DoS attacks or other non-networking equipment that is causing conflicts (such as wireless telephones, wireless security cameras, amateur TV (ATV) systems, RF-based remote controls, wireless headsets, microphones and audio speakers, and other devices that use the 2.4 GHz frequency).

Jamming Attacks

Jamming a wireless LAN is similar in many ways to how an attack would target a network with a DoS attack – the difference is that in the case of the wireless network, the attack can be carried out by one person with an overpowering RF signal.

The attacker does not need to gain access to your network; instead they can sit in your parking lot or even further away to execute the attack. Although you may be able to readily determine the fact that you are being jammed, you may find yourself hard pressed to solve the problem. Indications of a jamming attack include the sudden inability of clients to connect to APs where there was not a problem previously.

Jamming attacks are sometimes used as the prelude to further attacks. In some cases, you find that RF jamming is not always intentional and may be the result of other, nonhostile, sources such as a nearby communications tower or another wireless LAN that is also operating in the same frequency range. Baby monitors, cordless telephones, microwave ovens, and many other consumer products may also be sources of possible interference.

CONFIGURING WINDOWS CLIENT COMPUTERS FOR WIRELESS NETWORK SECURITY

Some wireless LAN security mechanisms are internal to Windows itself, while others are third-party solutions or part of the IEEE 802.11 standard.

- Windows XP Professional – provides excellent support for 802.11 wireless networks and 802.1x security to the mainstream.
- Windows Vista Business – very simple to connect to a wireless network and provides security for the connection.

SITE SURVEYS

A *site survey* is part of an audit done on wireless networks. Site surveys allow system and network administrators to determine the extent to which their wireless networks extend beyond the physical boundaries of their buildings. Typically, a site survey uses the same tools an attacker uses, such as a sniffer and a WEP cracking tool (for 802.11 network site surveys).

Summary of Exam Objectives

WLANs are inherently insecure because of their very nature; the fact that they radiate radio signals–containing network traffic that can be viewed and potentially compromised by anyone within range of the signal. With the proper antennas, the range of WLANs is much greater than is commonly assumed.

There are a number of different types of wireless networks that can be potentially deployed. These include HomeRF, Bluetooth, 802.11n, 802.11g, 802.11b, and 802.11a networks. The most common type of WLAN in use today is based on the IEEE 802.11g standard.

The 802.11 standard defines the 64-bit Wired Equivalent Privacy (WEP) protocol as an optional component to protect wireless networks from eavesdropping. WEP is insecure because it encrypts well-known and deterministic IP traffic in layer 3, and it is vulnerable to plaintext attacks. That is, it is relatively easy for an attacker to figure out what the plaintext traffic is (for example, a DHCP exchange) and compare that with the ciphertext, providing a powerful clue for cracking the encryption.

Another problem with WEP is that it uses a relatively short (24-bit) IV to encrypt the traffic and WEP uses RC4 as the encryption algorithm, which is well known and recently it was discovered that it uses a number of weak keys. AirSnort and WEPCrack are well-known open-source tools that exploit the weak key vulnerability of WEP. The response to the weaknesses in WEP is the use of Wi-Fi Protected Access (WPA) which has a longer IV, a stronger algorithm, and a longer key.

MAC filtering is another defensive tactic that can be employed to protect wireless networks from unwanted intrusion. Only the wireless station that possess adaptors that have valid MAC addresses are allowed to communicate with the AP. However, MAC addresses can be easily spoofed and maintaining a list of valid MAC addresses may be impractical in a large environment.

Top Five Toughest Questions

1. You are a corporate user trying to connect to the company's wireless network. When you look at the list of available networks, you do not find the corporate network listed. What is most likely the cause?
   A. Wireless is turned off
   B. Incorrect mode
   C. Beaconing is turned off
   D. Interference

2. You are a corporate user trying to connect to the company's wireless network. You are within the distance limit of the wireless network yet you

are unable to find the network. When you move closer, the network then shows up. What could be the cause?

A. Structural interference between the access point and your machine

B. Environmental interference such as electromagnetic interference

C. Radio frequency interference from other devices

D. All of the above

3. You are a corporate user trying to connect to the company's wireless network. When you attempt to connect to the network, you are denied being able to connect, what could be the cause?

A. Wrong 802.11 standard

B. Incorrect encryption type

C. Bad username

D. Interference

4. You are a user in a company who would like to connect to the company's wireless network. The company uses access points for connection to the corporate LAN. To what mode should your wireless connection be set to attach to WAPs?

A. Ad Hoc

B. Secure

C. Infrastructure

D. WPA

5. You are running a wireless network using 802.11g. You fear that someone might eavesdrop on your confidential information. What protocols could you use to protect your wireless network?

A. WPA

B. 802.1X

C. WEP

D. Multiple Input/Multiple Output (MIMO)

Answers

1. Correct answer and explanation: **C.** To protect wireless networks, often the SSID is not beaconed or sent out so wireless users can see it. To connect to this type of network, you must choose to connect manually, type in the SSID and choose to connect even if the SSID is not broadcasting.

Incorrect answers and explanations: **A**, **B**, and **D**. Answer **A** is incorrect because wireless is working for other users so this would not be the case. Answer **B** is incorrect because computers can choose automatically between infrastructure and ad hoc. Answer **D** is incorrect because interference would not cause the network to not show up.

2. Correct answer and explanation: **D.** All of these could be a problem. Structural interference such as thick walls, metal between the access point and computer could cause a shortening of distance. EMI environmentally

could cause a shortening of distance. RFI could also cause a shortening of distance.

3. Correct answer and explanation: **B**. If the wireless networking devices are not setup for the same encryption, then the connection will be denied.

   Incorrect answers and explanations: **A, C,** and **D**. Answer **A** is incorrect because if you can see the network, then you are using the same 802.11 standard. Answer **C** is incorrect because usernames are only used with RADIUS authentication. Answer **D** is incorrect because interference would not cause the denied connection.

4. Correct answer and explanation: **C**. When you connect to wireless access points, your connection should be set for infrastructure mode.

   Incorrect answers and explanations: **A, B,** and **D**. Answer **A** is incorrect because Ad-Hoc is for computer to computer connection. Answer **B** is incorrect because though a secure connection would be good, this is not a mode for wireless connection Answer **D** is incorrect because WPA is an encryption protocol and not a mode.

5. Correct answer and explanation: **A** and **C**. The older of the wireless encryption protocols is WEP, and the newer version is called *WPA*.

   Incorrect answers and explanations: **B** and **D**. Answer **B** is incorrect because this is a wireless authentication protocol. Answer **D** is incorrect because this is used by 802.11n to achieve greater speeds.

CHAPTER 5

The OSI Model and Networking Protocols

Exam objectives in this chapter
- The OSI Model
- The Department of Defense Networking Model
- Networking Protocols

THE OSI MODEL

In 1977, the International Organization for Standardization formed a subcommittee called the *Open Systems Interconnection* (OSI) from which a seven-layered framework was established and is still used as the model for distributed communications. The OSI model is shown in Figure 5.1.

The first two layers of the OSI model involve both hardware and software. In the five upper layers (Layers 3 to 7), the OSI model typically is implemented via software only.

Crunch Time

The OSI model is represented as a stack because data that is sent across the network has to move through each layer at both the sending and receiving ends. The sending computer generally initiates the process at the application layer and the data is sent down the stack to the physical layer and across the network to the receiving computer. On the receiving end, the data is received at the physical layer and the data packet is sent up the stack to the application layer.

The application layer starts the process. Small pieces of information relative to the transmission of information are added to the data at each layer; this is called *encapsulation*. The process is then reversed on the receiving side to get back to just the data.

Layer 7 Application	
Layer 6 Presentation	
Layer 5 Session	
Layer 4 Transport	
Layer 3 Network	
Layer 2 Data Link	LLC
	MAC
Layer 1 Physical	

FIGURE 5.1
The OSI model

Layer 1: Physical

The first layer of the OSI model is the physical layer. This layer specifies the electrical and mechanical requirements for transmitting data bits across the transmission medium. It involves sending and receiving the data stream on the carrier – whether that carrier uses electrical (cable), light (fiber optic) or radio, infrared or laser (wireless) signals. The physical layer specifications include the following:

- Voltage changes
- Timing of voltage changes
- Data rates
- Maximum transmission distances
- Physical connectors to the transmission medium
- Physical topology or layout of the network

The physical layer addresses digital versus analog signaling, baseband versus broadband signaling, synchronously or asynchronously transmissions, and how signals are divided into channels (multiplexing).

EXAM WARNING

Modems translate analog to digital signals and back again. PCs are using digital technology to communicate, but the phone lines are using analog signaling. Therefore, the signal must be changed from one signaling method to the other as needed, such as when you want to connect your PC up to your Internet service provider (ISP) and surf the Internet.

Layer 2: Data Link

The data link layer is responsible for maintaining the data link between two hosts or nodes. Its characteristics and functions are as follows:

- Defines and manages the ordering of bits to and from data segments called *packets*
- Management of frames, which contains data arranged in an organized manner, which provides for an orderly and consistent method of sending data bits across the medium
- Responsible for flow control, which is the process of managing the timing of sending and receiving data so that it doesn't exceed the capacity of the physical connection
- Responsible for error notification, including receiving and managing error messaging related to physical delivery of packets
- Network devices that operate at this layer include Layer 2 switches (switching hubs) and bridges.
- The data link layer is divided into two sublayers:
  - **Logical Link Control (LLC) sublayer** provides the logic for the data link. Thus, it controls the synchronization, flow control, and error checking functions of the data link layer.
  - **Media Access Control (MAC) sublayer** provides control for accessing the transmission medium. It is responsible for moving data packets from one network interface card (NIC) to another, across a shared transmission medium. Physical addressing is handled at the MAC sublayer. MAC is also handled at this layer. This refers to the method used to allocate network access to computers and prevent them from transmitting at the same time, causing data collisions. Common MAC methods include Carrier Sense Multiple Access/Collision Detection (CSMA/CD), used by Ethernet networks, Carrier Sense Multiple Access/Collision Avoidance (CSMA/CA), used by AppleTalk networks, and token passing, used by Token Ring and Fiber Distributed Data Interface (FDDI) networks.

EXAM WARNING

A MAC address consists of six hexadecimal numbers. The highest possible hexadecimal number is FF:FF:FF:FF:FF:FF, which is a broadcast address. The first three bytes contain a manufacturer code and the last three bytes contain a unique station ID. You can view the MAC address on most systems with the following commands.

Windows ME, 9x: **winipcfg** (navigate the graphical user interface (GUI) to find the MAC address)

Windows NT, XP, Vista, 2000, 2003, 2008: **ipconfig/all**

Linux: **ifconfig -a**

Layer 3: Network

At the network layer, packets are sequenced and logical addressing is handled. Logical addresses are nonpermanent, software-assigned addresses that can be changed by administrators. The IP addresses used by the Transmission Control Protocol/Internet Protocol (TCP/IP) on the Internet and the Internetwork Packet Exchange (IPX) addresses used by the IPX/Sequenced Packet Exchange (SPX) protocols on NetWare networks are examples of logical addresses. These protocol stacks are referred to as routable because they include addressing schemes that identify both the network or subnet and the particular client on that network or subnet. Each subnet must be unique, and each local area network (LAN) will need to know how to get to the other LANs. Routing refers to forwarding packets from one network or subnet to another. Logical addressing is important since it defines how and where the packets are sent. Its characteristics and functions are as follows:

- A TCP/IP called *Address Resolution Protocol* (ARP) helps map an IP address to a physical machine address.
- This is the first layer responsible entirely for the logical connection between two hosts, not the physical one.
- It defines the mechanisms used to route packets between networks. Without these Layer 3 functions, only local communications would be able to take place.
- It provides additional levels of flow control and error control.
- The devices that operate at this layer include, most prominently, routers and Layer 3 switches.

Layer 4: Transport

The transport layer is responsible for transporting the data from one node to another, and it provides transparent data transfer between nodes and manages the end-to-end flow control, error detection, and error recovery.

The transport layer protocols initiate contact between host computers and set up a virtual circuit. The transport protocols on each host computer verify that the application sending the data is authorized to access the network and that both ends are ready to initiate the data transfer. When this synchronization is complete, the data can be sent. As the data is being transmitted, the transport protocol on each host monitors the data flow and watches for transport errors. If transport errors are detected, the transport protocol can provide error recovery.

Its characteristics and functions are as follows:

- It is responsible for providing reliability and connection-oriented or connectionless communications.
- The two protocols most commonly associated with the transport layer are the TCP, which is connection-oriented, and the User Datagram Protocol (UDP), which is connectionless.
- It handles ports, which are another aspect of logical addressing. Ports are used to determine which incoming data belongs to each application running on a particular host.
- It is responsible for name resolution.

Layer 5: Session

The session layer is responsible for establishing, monitoring, and terminating sessions, using the virtual circuits established by the transport layer. Its characteristics and functions are as follows:

- It is responsible for putting header information into data packets to indicate where the message begins and ends.
- It performs synchronization between the sender's session layer and the receiver's session layer. The use of acknowledgement messages (ACKs) helps coordinate transfer of data at the session layer.
- It controls whether the communications within a session are sent as full duplex or half duplex messages.
- It establishes a connection between two processes. A *process* is a defined task related to an application.
- The session layer is responsible for setting up the connection between an application process on one computer and an application process on another computer, after the transport layer has established the connection between the two machines.
- Protocols that operate at the session layer include Windows Sockets (the Winsock interface) and the Network Basic Input/Output interface (NetBIOS).

Layer 6: Presentation

In the presentation layer, data translation is the primary activity performed. The sender's application passes data down to the presentation layer, where it is put into a common format. When the data is received on the other end, the presentation layer changes the data from the common format back into a format that is useable by the application. Protocol translation, the conversion of data from one protocol to another so that it can be exchanged between computers that use different platforms or operating systems, takes place here. Its characteristics and functions are as follows:

- Gateway services operate at this layer. Gateways are connection points between networks that use different platforms or applications.
- It is responsible for data compression, which is used to minimize the actual number of bits that must be transmitted on the network media to the receiver.
- It is responsible for data encryption and decryption.

Layer 7: Application

The application layer is the point at which the user application program interacts with the network. This layer of the OSI model should not be confused with the application itself. Application processes are initiated within a user application and then the data created by that process are handed to the application layer of the networking software. Everything that occurs at this level is application-specific. File sharing, remote printer access, network monitoring and management, Remote Procedure Calls (RPCs), and all forms of electronic messaging occur at this level.

Samples of application layer protocols are File Transfer Protocol (FTP), Telnet, Simple Mail Transfer Protocol (SMTP), Post Office Protocol 3 (POP3), Internet Message Access Protocol 4 (IMAP4), Hypertext Transfer Protocol (HTTP), Network News Transfer Protocol (NNTP), and Simple Network Management Protocol (SNMP). Be sure to distinguish between the protocols mentioned and applications that may bear the same names. For instance, there are many different FTP programs made by different software vendors, but all of them use the FTP protocol to transfer files.

EXAM WARNING

Knowing the OSI model is imperative. You will need to know which devices and protocols function at each layer, so you need to know the layers to start with. Continue to draw the model shown in Figure 5.1 so that when you get to the exam, you can write it on scrap paper to help you with the exam.

The Microsoft Model

With the release of Windows NT 3.1, TCP/IP was built into the operating system, providing a seamless integration of networking functionality in the OS. Since that time, it has become standard to provide TCP/IP with the operating system since so many computers today connect to a network in one form or another.

DID YOU KNOW?

The Microsoft model provides a standard platform for application developers. This modular design enables the developer to rely upon the underlying services of the OS through the use of standard interfaces. These interfaces provide specific functionality developers that can be used as building blocks to develop an application. This makes development time shorter and provides common interfaces for users, making learning and using new applications easier.

UNDERSTANDING THE FUNCTION OF BOUNDARY LAYERS

The Microsoft model describes software and hardware components and the connections between them that facilitate computer networking. This modular approach both allows and encourages hardware and software vendors to develop products that work together through the Microsoft operating system. Boundary layers are interfaces that reside at the boundaries of functionality. They interact with the layer below and the layer above, providing an interface from one layer to the next.

The interfaces defined by Microsoft are as follows:

- **Network Device Interface Specification (NDIS)** This layer maps to the data link layer of the OSI model and the network interface layer of the Defense Advanced Research Projects Agency (DARPA) model, which we will cover next. The NDIS layer is the boundary between the physical network and the higher level transport protocols. This layer provides the standardized functions that allow various transport protocols to use any network device driver that is compatible with the specifications of this layer, providing both flexibility and reliability to developers.
- **Transport Driver Interface (TDI)** This layer provides a portal into the transport protocols for kernel mode components such as servers and redirectors. It acts as the gateway between the transport layer and the session layer in the OSI model, providing a common interface, which developers can use to access both transport and session layer functionalities.
- **Application Program Interface (API)** This layer is the interface through which developers can access network infrastructure services such as various application layer protocols.

The Windows OS is divided into three primary areas: the User, the Executive, and the Kernel. The Kernel is the core of the Microsoft operating system architecture, and it manages the most basic operations, including interacting with the hardware abstraction layer that interacts with the hardware (CPU, memory, and so forth). The Kernel also synchronizes activities with the Executive level, which includes the Input/Output (I/O) Manager and the Process Manager. The User level interacts with the Executive level; this is the level at which most applications and user interfaces reside.

Figure 5.2 shows the relationship of these boundary layers to both the OSI model and to the Microsoft architecture.

THE DEPARTMENT OF DEFENSE NETWORKING MODEL

The DARPA architecture, known as the *DARPA model* or the *Department of Defense (DoD) model*, defines four layers starting at the network cable (or interface) and working its way up.

Each layer is designed with a specific function, and together they provide the foundation for internetworking. Different protocols within the TCP/IP suite work at different layers, as you'll discover when we examine the individual components of the TCP/IP suite.

Layer 1: Network Interface

Layer 1 in the DoD model is the network interface layer and it corresponds to the lowest level of the TCP/IP architecture correlating to Layers 1 and 2 in the OSI model. Figure 5.3 shows the mapping of layers from the OSI model to DoD

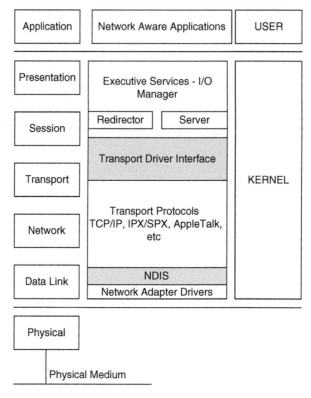

FIGURE 5.2
The Microsoft model

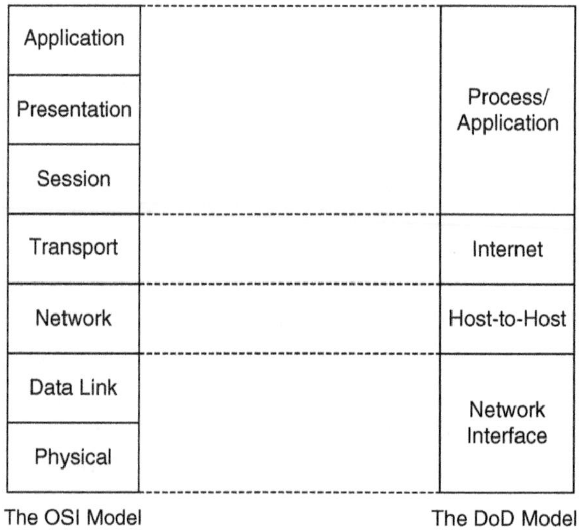

FIGURE 5.3
Mapping the OSI model
with the DoD model

model. The network interface layer provides most of the capabilities provided for in the physical and data link layers of the OSI model. This layer defines specifications for the lower level networking technologies; that is, those at the physical layer (NIC, connectors, and cables) and at the data link layer (access methods).

Hardware involved in the network at the network interface level are as follows:

- Network medium, which can be coaxial, fiber optic or twisted-pair cabling, or wireless networking
- NIC, which has both a physical MAC address and a logical IP address.

MEDIA ACCESS CONTROL

MAC refers to the method used to allocate use of the medium among the computers and devices on the network. In networking, access control is important since many devices share a common medium, such as a coaxial cable or twisted-pair cable.

Access control method lays out rules defining how access is allocated and is performed by MAC layer protocols. The most common access control methods today are:

- Carrier Sense Multiple Access with Collision Detection (CSMA/CD)
- Carrier Sense Multiple Access with Collision Avoidance (CSMA/CA)
- Token passing

NETWORK INTERFACE HARDWARE/SOFTWARE

The network interface is established through the NIC, which employs both hardware and software in connecting the device to the network media. Each type of NIC uses a different type of connector to connect to the physical medium. The connector types are delineated in the IEEE 802 specifications. The three most prominent are Ethernet, which is defined in 802.3, Token Ring, defined in 802.5, and wireless networking defined in 802.11.

The TCP/IP network interface layer defines protocols used by the NIC to receive, assemble, address, and transmit. The Ethernet NIC is also responsible for receiving/sending and assembling/disassembling data to and from the network connection. The network interface layer in the DoD model encompasses the functions of the OSI model's physical and data link control layers and controls media access and the assembly/disassembly of data at the lowest level of the hierarchy.

EXAM WARNING

For the Network+ exam, it's imperative that you understand the Institute of Electrical and Electronics Engineers, Inc. (IEEE) 802 model and its specific standards. Focus on the newer ones affecting today's current technologies, such as Ethernet, wireless, and security. Most significantly, Ethernet is defined in 802.3, Token Ring in 802.5, and wireless networking in 802.11.

The standards vary depending on the network technology, but because TCP/IP works independently of network technology, it can be used with networks such as Ethernet, Token Ring, Asynchronous Transfer Mode (ATM), and Frame Relay interchangeably.

Layer 2: Internet

Layer 2 in the DARPA model is the Internet layer, which maps to the network layer of the OSI model. The Internet layer is responsible for packaging, addressing, and routing the data.

Before data can be sent out over the network interface, it must have a standard format, size, and addressing scheme. The network interface layer is responsible only for taking the data it is given and translating it into signals on a physical medium. The Internet layer defines packet structure (what each bit of a data segment means), addressing, and routing.

Layer 3: Host-to-Host

Layer 3 in the DARPA model is the host-to-host transport layer, sometimes called the transport layer since this layer maps to the transport layer (Layer 4) in the OSI model. This layer is responsible for transporting the data and setting up communications between the application layer and the lower layers. It also is responsible for setting up the connection between hosts so that formatted data can be sent.

Because this layer establishes a connection, it can also take on some of the responsibilities of the session layer of the OSI model. In TCP/IP, the two core protocols used at the host-to-host transport layer are TCP and UDP.

Layer 4: Application

The application layer of the DARPA model operates at the session, presentation, and application layers of the OSI model. One of the main reasons why the DoD model is still used when referencing TCP/IP is because the TCP/IP protocol suite's protocols (such as FTP and Telnet) do not map perfectly into the OSI model, they have overlap, and this is why you will see three OSI model layers under one layer in the DoD model.

The DoD model's application layer enables applications to communicate with one another and it provides access to the services of the other underlying layers. In this way, developers do not have to write code continually to provide the underlying functionality but can simply access that functionality by adhering to agreed-upon standards and specifications.

NETWORKING PROTOCOLS

In this section, we will review some of the more common networking protocols in existence today.

- NetBIOS over TCP
  - NetBIOS over TCP (NetBT) is a legacy protocol and naming service.
  - It is a set of protocols that provides *name*, *session*, and *datagram* services for NetBIOS-based applications.

- NetBT name service allows host computers to attain and retain a NetBIOS name.
- It assists hosts in locating other computers with a specific NetBIOS name.
- The name service resolves a specific NetBIOS name to an IP address. This process utilizes broadcast messages that are sent to all hosts on the network. The name service uses UDP Port 137.
- NetBT session service provides for the reliable exchange of messages between two NetBIOS applications, typically on two different computers. The session service uses TCP Port 139.
- NetBT datagram service within NetBT provides connectionless, unreliable message delivery between NetBIOS applications via UDP Port 138.
- Windows Internet Name Service (WINS)
  - A NetBIOS name server allows the clients to attain, register, and resolve NetBIOS names.
  - WINS is specific to Microsoft networks and is not used on non-Microsoft operating system-based computers.
  - WINS creates a database where it stores name-to-IP address matches and it provides resolution services of these names to IPs in response to client queries.
  - It can replicate its database of NetBIOS names to other WINS servers to make name resolution services available across a large network.
  - NetBIOS name resolution uses four different node types to resolve names to IP addresses: Broadcast (B-node), Peer-to-peer (P-node), Mixed (M-node), and Hybrid (H-node).
  - The LMHOST file is a plain text file which is unique to Windows-based computers and contains a mapping of computer's NetBIOS name with an IP address. This static file was used prior to the implementation of dynamic NetBIOS name resolution found in WINS.

EXAM WARNING

NetBIOS name resolution can be done via a centralized WINS server or via a local LMHOSTS file, both of which are more efficient then broadcasting to map a NetBIOS name to an IP address, and will assist in keeping traffic down on your network.

- Server Message Block/Common Internet File System
  - The Server Message Block (SMB) Protocol was primarily used for file and print sharing, but it is also used for sharing serial ports and abstract communications technologies such as named pipes and mail slots.
  - SMB is also now known as *Common Internet File System* (CIFS); both names are used interchangeably.
  - CIFS is a protocol that is operating system-independent.
  - It is not TCP/IP dependent. The connection from client-to-server can be made via NetBEUI or IPX/SPX.

- Internet Printing Protocol
  - It provides the capability to perform various printing operations across the network using HTTP, version 1.1.
- Windows Sockets
  - It is a Microsoft Windows API that provides a standard programming interface for accessing TCP/IP in Windows.
  - A number of built-in Windows tools rely on Windows Sockets, including ping and tracert.
- Telnet
  - It is a terminal emulation protocol that allows you to log onto a remote computer.
  - The remote computer must be using TCP/IP and have the Telnet server service running.

EXAM WARNING

Remember that Telnet uses port 23 (both TCP and UDP) for communication; Secure Shell (SSH) (essentially encrypted Telnet) runs on port 22 (also TCP and UDP). Telnet information is sent in plaintext so it's very easy to capture packets and read the contents such as usernames and passwords. SSH, on the other hand, encrypts all communications between the hosts.

- Dynamic Host Configuration Protocol
  - It is used to automatically assign IP addresses to host computers on a network running TCP/IP.
  - It automatically maintains a database of the assigned addresses, ensuring that there will never be duplicate addresses among the Dynamic Host Configuration Protocol (DHCP) clients.
- Simple Mail Transfer Protocol
  - It is a protocol used to send e-mail messages and attachments between servers and from clients to servers.
  - SMTP operates at the application layer and relies on the services of the underlying layers of the TCP/IP suite to provide the actual data transfer services.
  - Remember that SMTP uses port 25 for communication
- Post Office Protocol
  - It is a widely used e-mail protocol that is used to retrieve e-mail from an e-mail server for the client application.
  - The current version of POP is POP3.
  - Remember that POP3 uses port 110 for communication.
- Internet Message Access Protocol
  - It is an e-mail protocol used to retrieve e-mail from a server.
  - The client program can access the mail and allow the user to read, reply to, and delete it while it is still on the server.
  - Remember that IMAP4 uses Port 143 (both TCP and UDP) for communication.

- Hypertext Transport Protocol
    - It is a protocol used to transfer files used on the Internet to display Web pages.
    - It uses port 80 for communication.
    - Utilizing Secure Sockets Layer (SSL) traffic may be encrypted and transmitted across port 443. This is known as *HTTP Secure* (HTTPS).
- Network News Transfer Protocol
    - It allows servers and clients to exchange information in the form of news articles.
    - NNTP is implemented as an application layer client/server protocol.
    - Remember that NNTP uses port 119 for communication.
- File Transfer Protocol
    - It is a protocol used to transfer files from one host to another, regardless of the hosts' physical locations.
    - One of the problems with FTP is that it transmits users' passwords in clear text, so it is not a secure protocol.
    - Two separate connections are established for an FTP session. Command information is transmitted over TCP port 21 while the actual data is sent over TCP port 20.
- Domain Naming System
    - It is used to resolve a host name to an IP address to facilitate the delivery of network data packets.
    - It is the protocol used on the Internet to resolve host names to IP addresses.
    - The HOSTS file is a plain text file which contains a mapping of computer's host name with an IP address. This static file was used prior to the implementation of Domain naming system (DNS) for name resolution.
    - Remember that DNS uses port 53 (both TCP and UDP) for communication.
- Routing Information Protocol
    - It is used to exchange routing information among IP routers.
    - Routing Information Protocol (RIP) is a basic routing protocol designed for small- to medium-sized networks. It does not scale well to large IP-based networks (including the Internet).
    - RIP uses port 520.
- Network Time Protocol
    - It is a protocol that provides a method for transmitting and receiving an accurate time source over TCP/IP-based networks.
    - Remember that Network Time Protocol (NTP) uses port 123 for communication. Do not confuse this with NNTP, which uses port 119.
- Simple Network Management Protocol
    - It is used for communications between a network management console and the network's devices, such as bridges, routers, and hubs.
    - SNMP employs a management system/agent framework to share relevant network management information.

- Information is stored in a management information base (MIB) and contains a set of objects, each of which represents a particular type of network information such as an event, an error, or an active session.
- SNMP employs UDP datagrams to send messages between the management console and the agents.

Summary of Exam Objectives

In this chapter, we covered the OSI model, the Microsoft model, and the DoD model, all of which are similar, share common core elements, but have differences as well.

From the DARPA experiment came the understanding that networking would become increasingly common and increasingly complex. The OSI model was developed, based on the original DARPA model, and approved by the OSI subcommittee of the ISO. The OSI model defined seven layers for standard, reliable network communications: physical, data link, network, transport, session, presentation, and application.

The physical layer is responsible for signaling, transmission medium, and ones and zeros traversing the wire. The next layer, the data link layer, is where your MAC address is located. On Ethernet NICs, the physical or MAC address (also called the hardware address) is expressed as 12 hexadecimal digits, arranged in pairs with colons between each pair, for example, 12:3A:4D:66:3A:1C. In binary notation, this translates to a 48-bit (or 6-byte) number, with the initial three bytes representing the manufacturer and the last three bits representing a unique NIC made by that manufacturer. The data link layer is subdivided into two sub layers known as the LLC and MAC layer. The LLC sub layer is responsible for providing the logic for the data link, and thus, it controls the synchronization, flow control, and error checking functions of the data link layer.

The TCP/IP suite provides the functionality specified in the OSI model using the four-related layers of the DoD model: network interface, Internet, host-to-host, and application. The network interface layer maps to the physical and data link layers of the OSI model and the Internet layer maps to the OSI network layer. The host-to-host layer maps to the OSI transport layer and DoD's application layer maps to the session, presentation, and application layers of the OSI model. Some of the more commonly known application layer protocols are FTP, HTTP, POP3, WINS, DNS, and DHCP.

Understanding the details of the TCP/IP suite is fundamental to managing computers in today's networked environment. Being able to subnet, assign IP addresses, create subnet masks, and set up routing are essential skills you'll need on the job and to successfully master the material on the Network+ exam.

Top Five Toughest Questions

1. You are the system administrator for a small company that runs two Windows servers (Windows Server 2003) and two Linux servers (SUSE Linux).

You need to lock down the connections to the switch via port security; this essentially means you will need to retrieve the MAC addresses on the systems. MAC addresses are found on Linux server by issuing which command?
A. ipconfig/a
B. ifconfig/a
C. winipcfg/a
D. ifconfig-a

2. You are a network administrator looking to implement technology into a company. You are told you need to build a network utilizing the IEEE 802.11 standard. From the list below, the IEEE 802.11 standard maps to which of the following? (Select only one answer).
A. Token Ring
B. Wired Ethernet
C. Metropolitan Area Network
D. Wireless in Infrastructure mode

3. From the list of choices, which of the following media access methods is used for an IEEE 802.5 network?
A. Direct sequence
B. Token passing
C. CSMA/CD
D. CSMA/CA

4. Which of the following is a valid MAC address?
A. 00:05:J6:0D:91:K1
B. 10.0.0.1 – 255.255.255.0
C. 00:05:J6:0D:91:B1
D. 00:D0:A0:5C:C1:B5

5. Standards for CSMA/CD are specified by which IEEE 802 sublayer?
A. 802.1
B. 802.2
C. 802.3
D. 802.5

Answers

1. Correct answer and explanation: **D**. It is very easy to confuse the system commands as they are very similar. Ifconfig-a is the correct command to use with Linux systems in order to view the MAC addresses.

   Incorrect answers and explanations: **A**, **B**, and **C**. Answer **A** is incorrect, it depicts the Windows command ipconfig. Answer **B** is incorrect, ifconfig is the correct command to use with Linux systems, however the switch depicted in this answer is incorrect. Answer **C** is incorrect, it depicts the Windows command winipcfg.

2. Correct answer and explanation: **D**. 802.11 Standards such as 802.11, 802.11b, 802.11a, and 802.11g are related to wireless networking.

Incorrect answers and explanations: **A**, **B**, and **C**. Answer A is incorrect, Token Ring maps to the 802.5 standard. Answer B is incorrect, Wired Ethernet maps to the 802.3 standard. Answer C is incorrect, Metropolitan Area Network (MAN) maps to the 802.6 standard.

3. Correct answer and explanation: **B**. The 802.5 standard defines a Token Ring network. Token Ring uses token passing as its method of communicating on the network.

Incorrect answers and explanations: **A**, **C**, and **D**. Answer A is incorrect, direct-sequence is a HYPERLINK "http://en.wikipedia.org/wiki/Modulation" ø "Modulation" modulation technique used by telecommunication technologies. Answer C is incorrect, CSMA/CD is used by Ethernet which maps to the 802.3 standard. Answer D is incorrect, CSMA/CA is used by wireless LANs which maps to the 802.11 standard.

4. Correct answer and explanation: **D**. A MAC address consists of six hexadecimal numbers. The highest possible hexadecimal number is FF:FF:FF:FF:FF:FF, which denotes a broadcast. The first three bytes contain a manufacturer code and the last three bytes contain a unique station ID. The numbers are counted from 0 to 9 and then lettered A to F before adding another digit. The letters A to F represent decimal numbers 10 to 15, respectively.

Incorrect answers and explanations: **A**, **B**, and **C**. Answer A is incorrect because a quick scan of the hex shows a letter "K" used, which is not in the base16 numbering system. Answer B is incorrect, because it is displaying the IP address format, which is based on binary. Answer C is incorrect, as a quick scan of the hex shows a letter "J" used, which is not in the base16 numbering system.

5. Correct answer and explanation: **C**. CSMA/CD is used on multiple access networks as defined in the IEEE 802.3 specification.

Incorrect answers and explanations: **A**, **B**, and **D**. Answer **A** is incorrect, 802.1does not utilize CSMA/CD. Answer **B** is incorrect, 802.2 does not utilize CSMA/CD. Answer **D** is incorrect, 802.5 does not utilize CSMA/CD.

CHAPTER 6
TCP/IP and Routing

Exam objectives in this chapter
- Transmission Control Protocol/Internet Protocol
- Understanding IP Addressing
- Understanding Subnet Masking
- Strategies to Conserve Addresses
- Multicast, Broadcast, and Unicast
- Understanding Basic IP Routing

TRANSMISSION CONTROL PROTOCOL/INTERNET PROTOCOL

Transmission Control Protocol/Internet Protocol (TCP/IP) is a suite of protocols; two of the components in the suite form the protocol's name: TCP and IP.

IP was developed as part of the TCP effort to provide logically addressed and structured networking. The primary role of IP is to provide logical addresses and support the routing of traffic to its destination.

Fast Facts

- The most fundamental aspect of IP is its addresses.
- Public IPv4 addresses are nearly exhausted.
- Efforts to expand the capacity of IP addresses have resulted in the next generation of the protocol, IP version 6 (IPv6).

- IP supports the ability to send to a group through multicasting.
- IP provides the network layer addressing and functions for the TCP/IP stack.
- Information is transported in IP packets, in which the header remains consistent in terms of size and fields.

IP Version 4

IP is responsible for addressing and delivery by providing a logical address scheme. The original version of IP, referred to as IP version 4 (IPv4), consists of 32 bits spread over four 8-bit octets, expressed in dotted decimal format. For example, a 32-bit address may look like this in binary:

```
00001010000010110000110000001101
```

To improve readability, the 32-bit IP address splits into four blocks of 8 bits like this:

```
00001010    00001011    00001100    00001101
```

Finally, each 8-bit block is converted to decimal and the decimal values are separated with periods or dots. The converted IPv4 address, expressed as a dotted decimal address, is:

```
10.11.12.13
```

All information transported over IP is carried in IP packets. Some components of a packet are as follows:

- **Version** 4-bit field that identifies the version of IP (4 or 6).
- **Header length** 4-bit field that indicates the length of the header, as the IPv4 header is a variable between 20 and 64 bytes.
- **Time to live (TTL)** Limits the number of hops the packet is allowed to transit. At each hop, a router decrements (reduces) this field, and when it reaches zero, the packet is removed from the network. This prevents packets from bouncing around a network indefinitely when there is some sort of routing problem.
- **Protocol** Indicates the next protocol (header) following the IPv4 header, such as TCP or User Datagram Protocol (UDP)
- **Header checksum** Maintains the integrity of the IPv4 header.
- **Source and destination address** (32-bit addresses) Identify the source and destination for this packet.

IP Version 6

IP version 6 (IPv6), if implemented fully in the future, will solve the address depletion problem. IPv6 addresses are 128-bit identifiers for interfaces and sets of interfaces, not nodes. Three general types of addresses exist within

IPv6: unicast, anycast, and multicast. Characteristics and benefits of IPv6 addresses are as follows:

- Expanded addressing moves us from 32-bit address to a 128-bit addressing method.
- IPv6 addresses are written as 32-hex digits, with colons (:) separating the values of the eight 16-bit pieces of the address in hexadecimal format:

  7060:0000:0000:0000:0006:0600:100D:315B

- IPv6 virtually eliminates the need for address translation as a means of accessing external networks due to aggregatable global unicast addresses which do not require address translation, when used to access external networks such as the Internet.
- In IPv6, five header fields are eliminated. IPv6 packets have a fixed header of 40 bytes in length.

> **TIP**
> For the Network+ exam, a firm understanding of the development of IPv6 and its differences over IPv4 (such as being able to identify an IPv6 address over an IPv4 address) will be sufficient.

UNDERSTANDING IP ADDRESSING

Each IP address contains two elements: the network address space or network ID and the host address space or host ID.

Fast Facts

Here are some key points related to converting from decimal to binary:

- The binary system relies on only two digits: 0 and 1.
- Each binary digit is called a *bit*, and in IP addressing, eight bits form an octet.
- Each octet has eight bits and a maximum value of 255.
- An IP address has four octets, or a total of 32 bits.
- Binary numbers are counted beginning with bit 0, the right-most bit, as shown in Table 6.1.
- To create a binary number, we set the desired bit to 1.
- To convert a binary number to decimal, add the value of each bit position set to 1.

Table 6.1	Decimal Values							
Bit number	Bit 7	Bit 6	Bit 5	Bit 4	Bit 3	Bit 2	Bit 1	Bit 0
Decimal value	128	64	32	16	8	4	2	1

For example, the binary value of 00101001 would be translated to: $32 + 8 + 1 = 41$.

Network ID and Host ID

A 32-bit IP address is subdivided into two portions, the network address (shared by all computers on that network) and the host address. See Figure 6.1 for an example of the division between the network and the host address. When combined, the result is a single unique IP address on the network.

Crunch Time

Be sure that you know these facts related to *network addresses*:

- All the hosts on the same network segment must have the same network ID.
- Primary network IDs are managed by the Internet Network Information Center (InterNIC).
- Network addresses are broken into classes: Class A, B, C, D, and E.
  - Classes A, B, and C are used for standard addressing.

- Class D is reserved for IP multicast addresses.
- Class E addresses are reserved for future use, and the class is considered experimental.
- A new classless (also called variable length subnet masking [VLSM]) system now exists. The class-based system now often is referred to as classful.
- We can identify the number of bits used for the network by notating how many total bits (counting from left to right) are used in the network address.

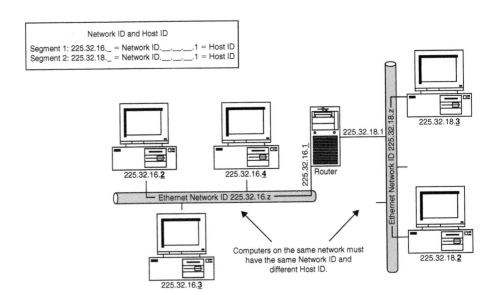

FIGURE 6.1
Network and host IDs

RULES FOR NETWORK IDS

The following rules apply for creating or using network IDs in a class-based system:

- Network IDs cannot begin with 127 as the first octet, since it is reserved for loopback address.
- A Network ID cannot have all bits set to 1. This configuration is reserved for broadcast addresses.
- A Network ID cannot have all bits set to 0. This configuration is reserved for indicating a host on the local network.
- A Network ID must be unique to the IP network.

Table 6.2 lists three network address classes.

RULES FOR HOST IDS

The following rules apply to creating and assigning host IDs:

- A Host ID cannot have all bits set to 1. This configuration is reserved for broadcast addresses.
- A Host ID cannot have all bits set to 0. This configuration is reserved for the expression of IP network IDs.
- A Host ID must be unique to the network on which it resides.

Table 6.3 lists host address classes.

Table 6.2	Network Address Classes			
Address Class	**Octets Used**	**First Network ID**	**Last Network ID**	**Number of Networks**
Class A	1	1.x.y.z	126.x.y.z	126
Class B	2	128.0.y.z	191.255.y.z	16,384
Class C	3	192.0.0.z	223.255.255.z	2,097152

Table 6.3	Host Address Classes			
Address Class	**Octets Used**	**First Host ID**	**Last Host ID**	**Number of Hosts**
Class A	3	w.0.0.1	w.255.255.254	16,777,214
Class B	2	w.x.0.1	w.x.255.254	65,534
Class C	1	w.x.y.1	w.x.y.254	254

UNDERSTANDING SUBNET MASKING

Large networks are subdivided to create smaller subnetworks. This process of segmenting is called *subnetting*, and most networks are divided into segments called *subnets*. *Supernetting* is the process of combining smaller networks into one larger network.

- A *subnet mask* is a 32-bit number that is to shield or mask certain bits.
- The number of host IDs on a network is variable, but the network ID must be the same for all hosts on a segment.
- The underlying concept of subnets and subnet masking involves a binary process called *bitwise ANDing*.

DID YOU KNOW?

Bitwise ANDing simply means that we are performing the logical AND function on each bit. The simple AND statements can be expressed as shown here. Rather than a mathematical plus function, this is a comparison between two (or more) values.

```
0 + 0 = 0
0 + 1 = 0
1 + 0 = 0
1 + 1 = 1
```

Notice that the logical AND function results in a 1 only when *both* inputs are 1; otherwise, the result is 0.

Default Subnet Mask

A subnet mask is a four-octet number used to identify the network ID portion of a 32-bit IP address. A default subnet mask is based on the IP address classes we discussed earlier and is used on networks that are not subdivided. A subnet mask is required on all class-based networks, even on networks that are not subnetted.

The default subnet masks are shown in dotted decimal format in Table 6.4.

Custom Subnet Mask

Subnetting is accomplished by using bits from the host address space for the network address space.

Table 6.4	Default Subnet Masks
IP Address Class	**Default Subnet Mask**
Class A	255.0.0.0
Class B	255.255.0.0
Class C	255.255.255.0

- The custom subnet mask, also called a *variable length subnet mask*, is used to identify the bits used for a network address versus the bits used for a host address.
- Custom subnet masks are used when subnetting or supernetting.

To determine the appropriate custom subnet mask, typically referred to simply as subnet mask, for a network, you must follow these steps:

1. Determine the number of host bits to be used for subnetting.
   a. Determine the maximum number of subnets required including consideration for future anticipated growth.
   b. Determine how many host bits are required to create the number of subnets.
   c. Add together the values of the left-most bits from the octets, yielding the highest network ID.
2. Determine the new subnetted network IDs.
   a. List all the possible binary combinations of the bits taken from the host address space.
   b. Calculate the incremental value to each subnet and add to the network address.
3. Determine the IP addresses for each new subnet.
   a. Start with counting out the default class network ID bits.
   b. Add the bits that were borrowed from the host ID to the default network ID.
4. Determine the appropriate subnet mask.
   a. Use bitwise ANDing to compare the bits of the IP address and the subnet mask.
   b. The result of the comparison is the network ID.

STRATEGIES TO CONSERVE ADDRESSES

The following three strategies assist with address conservation:

- **Classless interdomain routing (CIDR)** Instead of full Class A, B, or C addresses, organizations can be allocated subnet blocks.
- **Variable length subnet mask** Conserve IP addresses by tailoring the mask to each subnet and by assigning just the right amount of addresses to each subnet. VLSMs are used when implementing a CIDR addressing scheme for a network.
- **Private addressing** If a host is not communicating directly with hosts in the global Internet, public IP addresses are not needed. Public addresses would be used on the outside and private addresses for inside networks, while network address translation (NAT) is used to convert those private (inside) addresses to public (outside) addresses as required. Three address blocks are defined as private address blocks, for situations in which the host does not connect directly to the Internet.

- **10.0.0.0/8** Class A network address with the host ID range of 10.0.0.1 through 10.255.255.254.
- **172.16.0.0/12** Class B network address with a host ID range of 172.16.0.1 through 172.31.255.254.
- **192.168.0.0/16** Class C network address with the host ID range of 192.168.0.1 through 192.168.255.254.

Another use of private addressing is called *automatic private IP addressing* (APIPA). If a computer running Windows 98 or later is configured to obtain its address automatically from a dynamic host configuration protocol (DHCP) server and it cannot locate a DHCP server, it will configure itself using APIPA. The computer randomly selects an address from the 169.254.0.0/16 address range and then checks the network for uniqueness. If the address is unique, it will use that address until it can reach a DHCP server. If the address is not unique, it will randomly select another address from that range.

EXAM WARNING

You must know the private address ranges as well as the APIPA IP address range for the Network+ exam. Also, do not forget the reserved loopback Class A address of 127.0.0.0.

Considerations

The private address blocks can be used in any network at any time. However, devices using these addresses will not be able to communicate with other hosts on the Internet without some kind of address translation. Some benefits of using private addresses are as follows:

- **Number of addresses** There are plenty of addresses for most internal networking needs.
- **Security** Private addresses are not routable on the Internet. The translation from private to public addresses further obscures internal network information.
- **Renumbering** If using NAT, no readdressing of privately addressed networks is necessary to access public networks.
- **Network design** Treating private addresses as public addresses when allocating ensures that efficiency and design are maximized.

STATIC AND DYNAMIC ASSIGNMENTS
- **Static addressing** Addressing configured by going to the physical location of a node or connecting through remote administration to configure a usable IP address.
- **Dynamic addressing** Addressing configured by a central server, which allocates and tracks the usage of IP addresses in the network.

- **Bootstrap protocol (BootP)** A communications protocol that allows you to manage IP addressing usage centrally and to automate the assignment of logical addresses in an organization's network.
- **Dynamic host configuration protocol (DHCP)** A communications protocol, based on BootP, that allows you to manage IP addressing usage centrally and to automate the assignment of logical addresses in an organization's network.
- DHCP is responsible for handing out a subset of IP addresses that an administrator configures into what is called a *scope*.
- The scope contains the address space range that has been preconfigured to be issued to a requesting client.
- Uses the concept of a *lease*, which is an amount of time that a given IP address will be valid for a computer.
- DHCP supports reservations for machines that require a permanent IP address.
- Additional client configuration options are available with DHCP, for example, domain name service (DNS) address, Windows Internet name service (WINS) address, and default gateway.
- DHCP is a broadcast-based protocol.
- DHCP relay agents are used to pass the DHCP broadcast messages across routers. The configuration is commonly called an *IP helper address* in Cisco Systems-based routers. If the router cannot function as a relay agent, each subnet that has DHCP clients requires a DHCP server.

MULTICAST, BROADCAST, AND UNICAST

- **Multicasting** can be used to push data to multiple hosts simultaneously. Characteristics of multicasting are as follows:
  - Designed to handle traffic destined to multiple hosts.
  - Multicast traffic establishes a one-to-many type of transmission, sending one stream of traffic to each requesting broadcast domain.
  - The IP address that defines a multicast group is a Class D address (224.0.0.0 to 239.255.255.255).
  - Multicast addresses cannot be used as source addresses for any traffic.
  - A multicast address identifies a group of hosts sharing the same address.
  - Multicast addresses are not *assigned* to a device, rather, a device proceeds to listen for and receive traffic destined to a multicast group that it has joined by some process.
  - Multicasting is UDP-based.
  - A computer uses Internet Group Management Protocol (IGMP) to report its multicast group memberships to multicast routers.
  - IGMP is required to be used in host computers that wish to participate in multicasting.

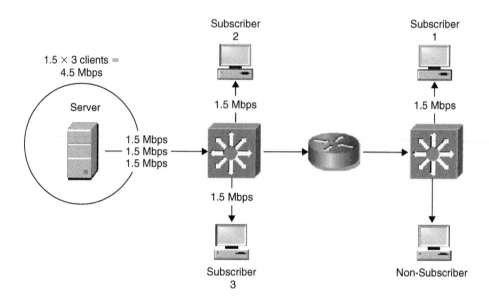

FIGURE 6.2
Unicast network video feed example

- **Unicast traffic** is the transmission of data from one host to another, one host at a time. Characteristics of unicast traffic are as follows:
  - A one-to-one session between one host and another, such as a client and server arrangement.
  - It will not transmit to every computer on a network.
  - Multiple requests for the same conference or data would cause that data to be pushed across the network media at the same time to multiple targets. An example of this is shown in Figure 6.2.
- **Broadcast traffic** is the broadcast traffic sent to all computer systems that can be reached on the network. Characteristics of broadcast traffic are as follows:
  - Each host receiving the broadcast has to process the broadcast traffic.
  - If a host does not require the broadcast traffic data, the host will still accept the datagram and then determine what to do with it – accept it or reject it.
  - Routers filter (block) broadcast traffic by default. Broadcasts must be explicitly allowed to traverse routers.

UNDERSTANDING BASIC IP ROUTING

As you prepare for the exam, be sure that you know the following key terms related to IP routing:

- **Routing** The process of sending a packet to its destination.
- **Router** A device that forwards packets from one network to another.
- **Gateway** A gateway connects one thing with another.

- **Direct delivery** The router is not used to forward the packet because the destination is on the same network (subnet or network segment) as the sending host.
- **Indirect delivery** Packets are sent to an intermediate point for forwarding, usually a router.

Crunch Time

How does a data packet travel from one host to another across the span of networks?

1. The sending host determines the destination IP address by using one of the name-to-IP resolution methods (WINS, DNS, and so forth).
2. The IP layer of a sending host consults with the routing table that is stored in memory.
3. Since the destination is on a different network, the packet will be sent by indirect delivery.
4. The address resolution protocol (ARP) table that is stored in memory is consulted to check for the existence of the required next hop media access control (MAC) address (MAC address of the local router in this case).
5. If the MAC is not in the ARP table, an ARP broadcast is sent to obtain the MAC address of the destination.

6. Then the packet is sent from the sending host with the data encapsulated in a frame format for the Network Interface Layer with the destination's physical address (MAC address of the router) included directly to the router.
7. The router takes a look at the packet and determines where it should be sent to reach its final destination.
8. The router passes the packet from its *internal interface* (the one with an address on the same subnet as the sender) to its *external interface* (the interface that's on a different subnet).
9. From there, the packet may make its way across many routers before reaching the subnet or network on which the destination computer resides.

IP Routing Tables

- Any IP node that initializes the TCP/IP stack will generate a default routing table based on the configuration of that node.

IP ROUTING TABLE ENTRIES

Routing table entries can be default, manual, or dynamic.

- The default values are created when the TCP/IP stack is initialized.
- Manual entries can be placed in the table for specific routes that may be desired. Some organizations, for instance, want specific traffic to go through specific routers. In that case, those routes can be entered into the routing table manually.
- Routes can be added dynamically if the router supports dynamic routing tables.

We'll discuss the differences between manual and dynamic routing in a moment. For now, let's look at the specific entries in a routing table. Routing table entries contain a number of elements in a specified order. Each of those elements is required and each is described briefly here.

- **Network destination** The network ID can be class-based, subnetted, or supernetted.
- **Netmask** The mask used to match the destination network with the IP address in the data.
- **Next hop or gateway** The IP address of the next router (a hop is one segment between routers. If a packet has to go through two routers, that would be two hops).
- **Interface** Identifies which network interface is used to forward the packet. Remember that every router has at least two interfaces.
- **Metric** The *metric* is a number used to help determine the best route for the packet. This typically is used to identify the route with the fewest hops. The metric is often expressed as the *cost of the route*.

Routing tables can also store four specific types of routes:

- **Directly attached network IDs** For packets destined for the local or attached network. If the sending and receiving hosts are both on the same subnet, for instance, the packet will be sent through this method.
- **Remote network IDs** Any packets destined for networks reachable through routers will be sent through this routing method.
- **Host routes** A *host route* is a route to a specific IP address. This type of route allows a packet to be sent to a specific IP address. The network ID is the IP address of the destination host and the network mask is 255.255.255.255.
- **Default route** The default route is used when a more specific network ID or route cannot be found. When all else fails, the default route is used. This is defined as a network ID of 0.0.0.0 and the network mask is 0.0.0.0.

Route Determination Process

Each IP packet has a destination IP address, which is used to determine how the packet will be routed. Using the logical ANDing process, the destination IP address and the subnet mask (or netmask) are compared. If they match, the packet stays on the local network and is sent directly to the destination IP address.

If the destination IP address and the subnet mask do not match, the entries in the routing table are compared with the destination IP address. If a match is found (that is, if the destination IP address and the subnet mask AND to a value found in the routing table), the packet is sent to the gateway listed in the routing table. If no matching entries can be found, the packet is sent to the defined default gateway. If more than one match is found in the routing table entries, the *metric* is used and the route with the fewest hops is typically selected. To view the route table on a Windows Server 2003 computer, access the command prompt, and type **route print**.

If there is no matching entry in the routing table, the packet will be sent to the default gateway for forwarding. When this process is complete, the resulting IP address (either destination IP address or gateway IP address) is then resolved to a physical address. This process uses ARP.

PHYSICAL ADDRESS RESOLUTION (USING ARP)

ARP resolves IP addresses to physical addresses. ARP is used to resolve the next-hop IP address to a physical MAC address using network broadcasts. The resolved MAC address is placed in the header of the packet as the destination MAC address.

DID YOU KNOW?

Just as a routing table is stored on the local host, so too is a list of the resolved IP-to-MAC addresses. This information is held in the *ARP cache*. Each time a request and resolution occur, both the sender and receiver store the other's IP-to-MAC address mapping. When a packet is received, the ARP cache is checked to see if the resolution has already been added to the cache. If so, the packet is immediately forwarded to the resolved address.

ARP process – The two steps in resolving an IP address to a MAC address are the *ARP request* and *ARP reply*. The format of the ARP request is a MAC-level broadcast that is sent to all nodes on the same physical segment as the sender. Whichever node sends the ARP request message is called the *ARP requester*. The node whose address matches the MAC address in the ARP request will respond by sending an ARP reply. This is a unicast (directly back to the sender only) MAC frame sent by the node called the *ARP responder*. The ARP responder's unicast message contains both its IP address and its MAC address.

- **Reverse ARP (RARP)** will resolve an IP address to a known MAC.
- **Inverse ARP (InARP)** is used to resolve the IP address on the other end of a virtual circuit.
- **Proxy ARP** occurs when one node answers ARP requests on behalf of another node. An ARP proxy device is often a routing device, but it does not act as an IP router.

STATIC AND DYNAMIC IP ROUTERS

Routing tables can be updated manually or dynamically. If the table must be updated manually, it is considered to be *static*. If the table can be updated automatically, it is considered to be *dynamic*.

Dynamic routing occurs when routing tables are automatically and periodically updated, and it relies upon routing protocols. Dynamic routing can be divided into two different classifications:

- **Interior gateway protocol (IGP)** is designed for routing within an autonomous system. The three most commonly used IP-based IGP routing protocols, are as follows:
  - **Routing information protocol (RIP)** is a *distance vector* routing protocol, and it determines routes based on the number of hops (how many routers

it must pass through). Any route which is more than 15 hops away is considered unreachable. More appropriate for small- to medium-sized networks.

- **Open shortest path first (OSPF)** is a *link state* routing protocol. Uses a method of dynamically updating routing information through link state advertisements (LSAs) that have information containing both the connected networks and their costs. The *cost* of each router interface is determined by the administrator to use best connections first. Appropriate for large networks.
- **Interior gateway routing protocol (IGRP)** is Cisco proprietary.
- **Enhanced interior gateway routing protocol (EIGRP)** is a Cisco proprietary hybrid protocol that combines the nest of advertisements in link-state protocols and the simplicity of distance vector.
- **Exterior gateway protocols (EGP)** are designed to control routing between autonomous systems. The three most commonly used IP-based EGP routing protocols are as follows:
  - **Border gateway protocol (BGP)** is a *distance vector* routing protocol, and it determines routes based on the number of hops (how many routers it must pass through).
  - **Intermediate system–intermediate system (IS–IS)** is a *link state* routing protocol. It uses a method of dynamically updating routing information through LSAs that have information containing both the connected networks and their costs. The *cost* of each router interface is determined by the administrator to use best connections first.

ROUTING UTILITIES

Four commonly used routing utilities are as follows:

- **Route** is used to view and modify the entries in the routing table.
- **Ping** is used to verify connectivity of intended destinations using Internet Control Message Protocol (ICMP) Echo messages.
- **Tracert** is used to send ICMP Echo messages to discover the path between a node and a destination.
- **Pathping** is used to discover the path between a host and destination or to identify high-loss links.

NETWORK ADDRESS TRANSLATION

NAT permits an organization's IP address structure to appear differently to outside networks than the actual address space it is using. It enables private IP networks that use nonregistered RFC1918 IP addresses to connect to the Internet. Characteristics of NAT are as follows:

- NAT allows hosts on a private network (inside network) to transparently communicate with destination hosts (outside network) in a global or public network by modifying the source address portion of an IP packet as it traverses the NAT device.

- The NAT device tracks each translation (conversation) between the source host (inside network) and the destination host (outside network), and vice versa and stores them in internal tables.
- Some router vendors call NAT tables as *translation tables.* Cisco calls them *xlate* on their PIX firewalls.
- NAT converts IP addresses from the private address space to the public address space.
- NAT is a method by which IP addresses are mapped from one address realm to another.
- This translation provides transparent routing from host to host.
- Port address translation (PAT) translates transport identifiers like TCP and UDP port numbers and ICMP query identifiers.

Summary of Exam Objectives

TCP/IP is a suite of protocols that provides the functionality specified in the OSI model using the four related layers of the Department of Defense model: network interface, Internet, host-to-host, and application.

IP addresses are 32-bit addresses represented in dotted decimal format (*w.x.y.z*). The 32 bits contain both a network and host ID. When sending data, the IP address in the packet is compared, using bitwise ANDing, to the subnet mask. The packet is sent to the appropriate internal or external location depending on the results of the ANDing process.

Network addresses were originally designed in a class-based system. Class A with an address range of 1.*x.y.z* to 126.*x.y.z*, Class B with an address range of 128.0.*y.z* to 191.255.*y.z*, and Class C with an address range of 192.0.0.*z* to 223.255.255.*z*. The default subnet masks are: Class A: 255.0.0.0; Class B: 255.255.0.0; and Class C: 255.255.255.0.

Classful networks can be subdivided into subnets using custom subnet masks. There is an inverse relationship between the number of subnets and the number of hosts per subnet.

Packets destined for networks that are not local are forwarded using gateways or routers. IP routing involves resolving the hostname or NetBIOS name to an IP address and resolving the IP address to a MAC address. NetBIOS name resolution uses four different node types to resolve names to IP addresses: broadcast (B-node), peer-to-peer (P-node), mixed (M-node), and hybrid (H-node). Names can also be resolved by using a HOSTS file or through the DNS or in the case of NetBIOS names with an LMHOSTS file or through WINS. The ARP is used to resolve the IP address to the MAC address that is unique to each Network Interface Card (NIC) manufactured.

Routing on a network can be static or dynamic. Four commonly used routing utilities are route, ping, tracert, and pathping. Protocols such as APIPA and DHCP help to get systems logically addressed dynamically. In this chapter, we also covered the use of protocol ports and the importance of them. You must memorize these port assignments for the Network+ exam.

Top Five Toughest Questions

1. You have been given an IP address in binary form. The address you have been given is 11000000.00000000.00000000.00000001. What is this IP address in decimal form?
   A. 127.0.0.1
   B. 191.0.0.1
   C. 137.0.0.1
   D. 192.0.0.1

2. You have been asked to explain what a certain IP address is used for. The IP address is 224.0.0.1. What are addresses in the 224.0.0.0 range used for?
   A. SNMP
   B. HTTP
   C. POP3
   D. Multicasting

3. You have a user who cannot get connected to the internet. You have the user run IPCONFIG/ALL and he reads you the IP address of 169.254.1.3. What is wrong with this system?
   A. System has a static IP address
   B. System has an APIPA address
   C. System has a bad address
   D. System has a classless address

4. A user has been given an IP address of 192.168.1.1 with a subnet mask of 255.255.255.0. How would you express the subnet mask for this address using CIDR notation?
   A. /24
   B. /8
   C. /16
   D. /22

5. A user has been given an address of fe80::9c5f:9695:f235:0051. What kind of address has she been given?
   A. IPV4 address
   B. IPV6 address
   C. MAC address
   D. Globally Unique Identifier (GUID)

Answers

1. Correct answer and explanation: **D**. You add $128 + 64$ for the first two ones to get 192.

   Incorrect answers and explanations: **A, B**, and **C**. Answer **A** is incorrect, 128 would be 01111111. Answer **B** is incorrect, 191 would be 10111111. Answer **C** is incorrect, 137 would be 100010011.

2. Correct answer and explanation: **D**. Addresses that begin with 224 are used for multicasting.

   Incorrect answers and explanations: **A, B**, and **C**. Answer **A** is incorrect, this is for network management. Answer **B** is incorrect, this is for browsing the web. Answer **C** is incorrect, this is for receiving e-mail.

3. Correct answer and explanation: **B**. The system has failed to get an IP address from a DHCP server and has assigned itself an automatic private IP address, which only allows for local communication.

   Incorrect answers and explanations: **A, C**, and **D**. Answer **A** is incorrect, the system would not have been assigned a static IP address in this range. Answer **C** is incorrect, this is a valid private APIPA address. Answer **D** is incorrect, classless addressing is not a factor in this problem.

4. Correct answer and explanation: **A**. The CIDR notation expresses how many bits are a part of the subnet mask. This address has 24 bits in the subnet mask.

   Incorrect answers and explanations: **B, C**, and **D**. Answer **B** is incorrect, this represents 255.0.0.0. Answer **C** is incorrect, this represents 255.255.0.0. Answer **D** is incorrect, this represents 255.255.252.0.

5. Correct answer and explanation: **B**. This is a condensed notation for a IPV6 address. The full address would be fe80:0000:0000:0000:9c5f:9695: f235:0051.

   Incorrect answers and explanations: **A, C**, and **D**. Answer **A** is incorrect, an IPV4 address looks like this, 192.168.1.1. Answer **C** is incorrect, a MAC address looks like this AA:BB:CC:DD:EE:FF. Answer **D** is incorrect, a GUID is used in Microsoft's Active Directory.

CHAPTER 7
Wide Area Networking

Exam objectives in this chapter
- What is a WAN?
- Switching Methods
- WAN Protocols and Properties
- Internet Access Methods

WHAT IS A WAN?

A wide area network (WAN) is a computer network covering a wide geographical area, including more than one remote location. The geographically dispersed locations are interconnected, thus forming a WAN.

Fast Facts

WANs may be created in different configurations, with the most common being some combination of public networks and private networks.

- Public networks are publicly accessed and connected to the Internet. They may use Internet Protocol Security (IPSec) or a virtual private network (VPN) to build a WAN over the Internet.

- Private networks are point-to-point network links, which are separated from the public Internet either physically or virtually. They may use Frame Relay or Multiprotocol Label Switching (MPLS) or a similar technology.

- A WAN covers a relatively broad geographic area and often uses transmission facilities provided by common carriers, such as telephone companies.

■ WAN technologies generally function at the lower three layers of the Open Systems Interconnection (OSI) model: the physical layer, the data link layer, and the network layer.

SWITCHING METHODS

WANs are based on one of two types of switching methods: *circuit switching* and *packet switching*.

Although almost all WAN protocols in use today are packet switched, there are still some old networks out there using circuit-switched technologies. Packet-switching technologies, such as X.25 and Frame Relay, are always available, so they do not have to be set up every time they are used. However, circuit-switching technologies are not. Circuit switching requires a separate setup for each connection session. This is the biggest difference between these two types of switching methods.

■ **Circuit switching** Circuit-switched networks are networks that are dialed on demand. The connection must be initiated before transmission can take place. Example: Integrated Services Digital Network (ISDN).
■ **Packet switching** Packet-switched networks are "always on." When you set the carrier's link up, it stays up. Examples: Frame Relay, asynchronous transfer mode (ATM), switched multimegabit data services (SMDSes), and X.25. Additional characteristics of packet-switched networks are as follows:
  ■ They divide the transmitting data into packets in which each is sent individually from the source to the destination.
  ■ All packets are given sequence numbers so that they can all be put back together again in the right order at the destination.
  ■ Each packet can take a different route to get to its destination.

EXAM WARNING

The telephone service provided by your carrier is most likely based on a circuit-switching technology. Circuit switching is ideal when data must be transmitted quickly and must arrive in the same order in which it's sent. Packet switching is the opposite of circuit switching. Packet switching is more efficient and robust, and it is commonly used for data that can withstand some delays in transmission.

WAN PROTOCOLS AND PROPERTIES

You must be able to understand and respond to questions about the speeds, capacity, transmission media, and distance for WAN protocols and standards such as terrestrial (T) carriers, ISDN, and *Fiber Distributed Data Interface* (FDDI).

In Europe and Japan, the corresponding carrier types are known as *E carriers* and *J carriers*, respectively.

- **T/E/J Carrier** The name T and the number following it denote the type of line.
  - T1 is a dedicated media connection supporting data rates of 1.544 Mbps. This speed is derived from 24 individual channels of 64 Kbps.
  - T3 can support data rates of about 43 Mbps, which is created with 672 channels of 64 Kbps.
  - E1 are European based and carry signals at 2 Mbps (32 channels at 64 Kbps, with two channels reserved for signaling and controlling).
  - E3 lines carry data at a rate of about 34.368 Mbps.
  - J lines are used within Japanese carrier systems.
  - T1 channels are sometimes known as *digital signal zero* (DS0s). In T-carrier systems, DS0 is a basic digital signaling rate of 64 Kbps, corresponding to the capacity of one voice or data channel.
  - Twenty-four DS0s (24 × 64 Kbps) equal one DS1. A full T1 is equal to a DS1; a full T3 is equal to a DS3.

EXAM WARNING

Make sure you are familiar with the speeds of the T- and E-carrier links, as well as the number of channels that make up a T1. T3 lines are faster than T1 lines because they have more bandwidth. Use common sense on the exam when determining which has a higher capacity. A T3 has a higher capacity than an E3, a T3 has a higher capacity than an E1, and so on. You may be asked to determine which line you would recommend based on the needs of the client, so be able to respond by knowing which technologies offer which benefits.

- **ISDN** ISDN is unique, in that it is call initiated and call terminated, so you only pay for what you use. ISDN uses telephone number-like entities called *service profile identifiers* (SPIDs) to dial from peer-to-peer to bring up the line when traffic has to be sent across it. Because of inactivity, the call is ended and so is the billing for that usage. There are two key access interfaces related to ISDN: *basic rate interface* (BRI) and *primary rate interface* (PRI).
  - BRI B channel service operates at 64 Kbps and is used for data; BRI D channel service operates at 16 Kbps and is used for signaling.
  - ISDN supports data transfer rates of 64 Kbps per channel, and most ISDN circuits used today are configured as two channels to provide 128 Kbps of throughput.
  - BRI consists of two 64 Kbps B channels and one D channel for transmitting control information. BRI ISDN has a maximum speed of 128 Kbps.
  - PRI consists of 23 B channels and one D channel (in North America) or 30 B channels and one D channel (in Europe). The B channel is used for control.

- In Europe, Australia, and other parts of the world, PRI provides 30 B channels plus one 64 Kbps D channel and a total interface rate of 2.048 Mbps.
- ISDN comprises digital telephony and data transport services offered by regional telephone carriers using preexisting telephone wiring.
- **FDDI** FDDI is debated to be a local area network (LAN) versus WAN technology. FDDI is generally used as a backbone technology due to its redundant design and high speed.
  - FDDI is based on fiber and is the standard for a 100 Mbps dual ring token passing technology.
  - It can also be based on copper cable, which is called *Copper Distributed Data Interface* (CDDI).
  - FDDI works using a dial ring token passing architecture that allows for bidirectional traffic – traffic traveling opposite directions – which is also called *counter rotation*.
  - FDDI and its primary and secondary rings are based on providing high-speed service reliably. The dual rings offer redundancy; in case of failure, the traffic can traverse the other link.
- **Frame Relay** Frame Relay is a packet-switching protocol for connecting devices on a WAN. Frame Relay is based on the older X.25 packet-switching technology, which was designed for transmitting analog data such as voice conversations, and is the skeleton for the MPLS solutions that are being used in most enterprises today.
  - Frame Relay networks in the United States support data transfer rates at T1 (1.544 Mbps) and T3 (45 Mbps) speeds and can be purchased as DS0s.
  - Frame Relay, when used in the WAN, is often used between a company's core and remote sites and can be sized perfectly to whatever bandwidth is needed between the sites.
  - Frame Relay allows for bursting which is when the carrier allows you to use some of the space on the rest of the whole line if available.
  - Frame Relay has a high transmission speed, very low network delay if configured properly and sized correctly, and it is fairly reliable.
- **MPLS** MPLS is a new WAN technology that is becoming very popular because of its many benefits, including its pure Layer 3 design and the fact that it is IP-based. Furthermore, MPLS allows you to label data to have a specific priority based on the application type. The quality of service (QoS) mechanisms in MPLS are quite sophisticated. MPLS is able to use labels to mark packets as they enter and exit the MPLS network. When the packets enter the MPLS network fabric, it is quickly routed to its destination based on its label and what that label specifies. MPLS operates at Layer 3 of the OSI model and is an excellent choice for voice and video applications. Request for Comments (RFC) 3031 (www.faqs.org/rfcs/rfc3031.html) shows many fine details on the inner workings of the technology and how MPLS operates.

Crunch Time

- At one time, X.25 was a popular standard for packet-switching networks, but new installations are few and far between these days.
  - X.25 is a WAN protocol that operates at Layers 1, 2, and 3 of the OSI model.
  - X.25 is very versatile, designed to operate in almost any environment. It is not as fast as other technologies but adds a very robust error-checking mechanism that virtually guaranteed error-free delivery of data. When network communications were carried on a much poorer network media than that we enjoy today, this was a very important protocol for WAN transmission.
- The terminology that stems from X.25 is still widely in use today. For example:
  - Packet-switching exchange (PSE)
  - Customer premises equipment (CPE)
  - Data circuit-terminating equipment (DCE)
  - Data terminal equipment (DTE)
- An X.25 network is primarily made up of these three groupings: DTE, DCEs, and PSEs.

- **Synchronous optical network** (SONET) SONET is an older, extremely high-speed network that provides a standard interface for communication carriers to connect networks based on fiber optic cable.
  - The SONET system uses fiber in dual counter-rotating rings.
  - The SONET is designed to handle multiple data types such as voice and video.
  - The SONET standard defines a hierarchy of interface rates that allow data streams at different rates to be multiplexed.
  - The SONET establishes optical carrier (OC) levels from 51.8 Mbps to 40 Gbps (as shown in Table 7.1). The OC is appended with a number, which indicates the speed of the medium. The base rate of OC-1 is 51.84 Mbps.

Table 7.1   Optical Carrier Levels and Data Transmission Rates

Optical Carrier Level	Data Transmission Rate
OC-1	51.84 Mbps
OC-3	155.52 Mbps
OC-12	622.08 Mbps
OC-24	1.244 Gbps
OC-48	2.488 Gbps
OC-192	10 Gbps
OC-256	13.271 Gbps
OC-768	40 Gbps

INTERNET ACCESS METHODS

In this section, we will look at Internet access technologies such as digital subscriber line (DSL), cable, Plain Old Telephone Service (POTS)/public switched telephone network (PSTN), satellites, and wireless.

Digital Subscriber Line

DSL is commonly denoted as xDSL, where the x specifies what type of DSL is in use. DSL is commonly used to access the Internet from both residential and business locations to provide high-speed access to the Internet. DSL became very popular as dial-up technologies become increasingly unable to meet the demand for fast access to the Internet.

- DSL and other high-speed technologies are slowly displacing dial-up service to the Internet. DSL is one of the most highly used because it can use preexisting phone lines in your home, so installation is a bit cheaper and less intrusive.
- DSL is not a shared medium, unlike cable networks, which use shared access. Shared access means that when there is heavy usage of the system, less bandwidth is available to individual users. DSL has dedicated bandwidth, so the only one using that bandwidth is you.

DID YOU KNOW?

One drawback of DSL, however, is that the QoS is dependent on the user's distance from the central office (CO).The CO is where the network endpoint is located and is generally run by your Internet service provider (ISP). The farther you are from the CO, the slower the service is. There are many forms of DSL. The most common forms of DSL are asymmetric DSL (ADSL) and symmetric DSL (SDSL).

ASYMMETRIC DSL

ADSL is the most widely deployed form of DSL technology. Most homes and small businesses currently using DSL technology use ADSL. Characteristics of ADSL are as follows:

- ADSL is used to transmit digital information on preexisting phone lines.
- Unlike dial-up, ADSL provides an always on connection to the Internet.
- ADSL is able to place voice and data information on the same line.
- ADSL is asymmetric. This means that ADSL is designed to provide more bandwidth in one direction than in the other.
- ADSL generates downstream speeds of about 8 Mbps and upstream speeds of up to 640 Kbps.

SYMMETRIC DSL

SDSL is typically used in larger companies, and the upstream and downstream channels have the same size; that is, the download speed and upload speed are equal. SDSL operates at about 2 to 2.5 Mbps.

EXAM WARNING

Other forms of DSL are very-high-speed digital subscriber line (VDSL), high-speed digital subscriber line (HDSL), symmetrical high-speed digital line subscriber (SHDSL), ISDN digital subscriber line (IDSL), and HDSL Second Generation (HDSL-2). You will have to be familiar with ADSL and SDSL not only for the exam but also for your own use if you plan to work on DSL. These are the most commonly used types and will surely be something you will want to know about in more depth if the situation arises where you may be working with this technology.

For the exam, you will need to know how to troubleshoot problems with DSL, although DSL itself may not be the problem. Look for misleading types of questions that ask you about DSL technology, although the questions are not essentially focused on that particular technology. The Network+ exam is notorious for these types of scenario questions. Be able to isolate what the cause of a problem may be, whether it be an ISDN, DSL, or WISP (wireless ISP) connection based on the technology and the underlying network – as well as problems may also be occurring there that are misleading you into the wrong answer. Finally, make sure that you remember that DSL and ISDN are both digital technologies, not analog.

Cable Modem

Broadband cable access requires the use of a modem designed to operate over cable TV lines. Because the coaxial cable used by cable TV provides much greater bandwidth than telephone lines, a cable modem can be used to achieve extremely fast access to the Internet. Cable modems are commonly used in small and home offices. Figure 7.1 shows a typical cable network setup.

Characteristics and features of cable modems are as follows:

- Cable networks provide a shared access to the users on the network, so heavy usage can slow it down, unlike DSL, which has dedicated user access.
- Because cable networks do not use preexisting phone lines in the home, cable companies will have to install a line into your home (at an additional cost) if one doesn't already exist.
- Cable networks provide speeds up to about 10 Mbps.
- Even with shared access, cable is often faster than ADSL.
- Cable networks are not available everywhere yet. DSL has more availability at this time than cable networks.

EXAM WARNING

Some of the most common questions that you are likely to have to solve will be in the form of how to troubleshoot network devices or which one is better and faster than the other. Which one should you use and for what reasons? Refer to Chapter 10, which discusses how to troubleshoot networking devices.

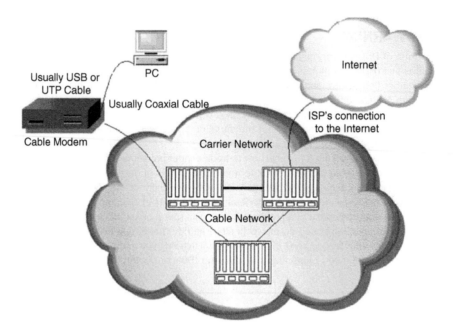

FIGURE 7.1
A typical cable network

Table 7.2	Typical Dial-Up Modem Speeds
Modem	**Speed**
V.90	56 Kbps (receive only)
V.34	33.6 Kbps
V.32 bis	14.4 Kbps

Plain Old Telephone Service/Public Switched Telephone Network

PSTN refers to the international telephone system based on copper wires carrying analog voice data. Telephone service carried by the PSTN is often called POTS, which refers to the standard telephone service that most homes use. When referring to either, we are generally referring to dial-up technologies where you would use a dial-up modem to connect to your ISP to get to the Internet. Table 7.2 lists typical dial-modem speeds.

Characteristics of POTS/PSTN are as follows:

- The speeds for dial-up are not very fast, providing speeds up to 56 Kbps.
- Dial-up is based on the telephone system and use analog lines, whereas both ISDN and DSL are digital.

Wireless

WISPs provide Internet access anywhere that it has coverage. Many locations that have very little access to a good last mile source utilize this technology to connect to the Internet. Homes also use this very often to get Internet access. You can access the Internet from an antenna in your local PC, no matter where you are, as long as you can access an antenna and have a clear shot to the antenna you want to connect with.

- **Wireless wide area network (WWAN)** WWANs are network traffic encapsulated in mobile communications technology such as Worldwide Interoperability for Microwave Access (WIMAX), Universal Mobile Telecom System (UMTS), code division multiple access (CDMA) 2000, Global System for Mobile (GSM), or 3G networks to name just a few. The mobile telecommunication cellular network allows users with WWAN cards or built-in cellular radios (GSM/CDMA) to surf the Web, send, and receive e-mail and in general perform any networking function as if physically connected to a WAN. Its characteristics are as follows:
  - Transmission rates are greatly reduced when compared with physical connections.
  - WIMAX is based on Institute of Electrical and Electronics Engineers, Inc. (IEEE) 802.16 standards or Broadband Wireless Access.
  - An acceptable rule of thumb is that WIMAX will sustain 70 Mbps transmission rates at approximately 30 miles.
  - As distance increases, throughput decreases and vice versa.
  - Competition for access point connectivity is reduced through scheduling such that once the WIMAX device connects to the access point, it is assigned a set time to communicate with the access point from then on.
- **Satellite** Satellite dishes are starting to gain popularity as a way to access the Internet. Many times (as is the case with cable), your carrier or ISP will provide you with television service or some other form of service, so you can use the satellite dish for multiple purposes. In addition, the dish is less intrusive into your home because it's mounted with very little need for wires or a run to a CO. A typical satellite-based network is shown in Figure 7.2. Characteristics of satellite are as follows:
  - A satellite is used to allow a user with a laptop, personal digital assistant (PDA), or PC with wireless satellite capabilities to connect to the Internet from anywhere within the coverage area.
  - It includes usage of low Earth orbit (LEO) and medium Earth orbit (MEO) satellites.
  - LEOs are primarily used with Internet-based satellite communications and are typically located at about 1,800 to 2,000 miles above Earth.
  - MEOs are located at about 9,000 to 10,000 miles above Earth.
  - There are also geosynchronous Earth orbits (GEOs), which are typically used for the carrier's or ISP's trunk lines.

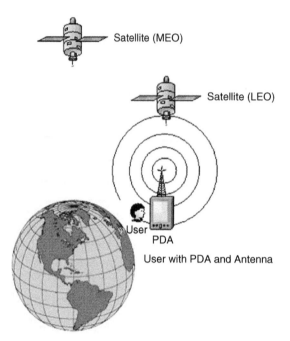

Satellite (MEO)

Satellite (LEO)

User
PDA

User with PDA and Antenna

FIGURE 7.2
A satellite-based network

- GEOs are located at about 22,000 to 23,000 miles above Earth.
- Wireless systems and satellites are commonly used in geographical areas that are far from a CO or when extreme flexibility is needed.

Summary of Exam Objectives

In this chapter, we covered the Network+ exam objectives based around wide area networking technologies such as packet switching, which is an "always on" network type, and circuit switching, which is an "on demand" network type. We also covered the fundamentals of ISDN, which is a digital method of transmitting data across copper telephone lines, using SPIDs to connect the network (circuit switched) for the sending and receiving of data. We covered the fundamentals of Frame Relay, MPLS, X.25, and SONET, as well as T- and E-level carrier lines.

We discussed the primary ways to get Internet access, such as with DSL. DSL is a digital method of transmitting data over preexisting copper telephone lines. ADSL is a technology that allows for faster download speeds. DSL speeds also vary depending on how far from the CO you are. Cable-based ISPs were also covered, which is generally faster than DSL but can also become congested if too many subscribers use the shared media all at once. Both are far better when it comes to speed and use than POTS or PSTN. The dial-up method of access using a standard modem is the slowest method of access. Satellite and WWAN technologies were also discussed; they afford you the flexibility of use over speed and security.

Top Five Toughest Questions

1. As the primary lead on your company's helpdesk, you are asked to help resolve a problem call with an ISDN line. A customer wants to upgrade an existing ISDN line because it's currently too slow. Right now, he is using a single BRI ISDN circuit switched B channel. From the available choices, what should his transmission rate be?

   A. 56 Mbps

   B. 64 Kbps

   C. 128 Kbps

   D. 256 Mbps

2. As the network administrator for your company, you are asked by your CIO to design and deploy a data link between two offices of your company. There are 10 employees located in each office. Your main concerns are the speed of the connections, the reliability of transferring of data, and the cost. Which solution should you implement? (Choose one.)

   A. Place a modem on a server in each office so that they can connect.

   B. Connect an ISDN circuit to each workstation in both locations.

   C. Use an ISDN circuit connected to a dedicated location or server in each building.

   D. Have each workstation at both locations and use a modem to connect to opposite offices.

3. As the Network Manager for rsnetworks.net, you need to implement a solution that will allow for sporadic connection to the Internet. Your only requirement is that you find a solution that will provide a connection of up to 128 Kbps to the Internet, only when needed. Which solution should you implement?

   A. T1

   B. T3

   C. 56 Kbps

   D. BRI ISDN

4. You are a network administrator at your company. Your company has a number of sales and marketing users who work remotely and telecommute from home or from sales meetings. These users dial into a Remote Access Server (RAS) to access the corporate headquarters. One day, one of the sales users dials up the RAS server to connect to the corporate headquarters network to access a few files. The sales user dials up the RAS server and cannot connect. The sales user when asked reports that there is no dial tone. What is the cause of the problem? (Choose one.)

   A. Telephone company problem

   B. The modem does not support the PC

   C. The modem settings are set incorrectly.

   D. There are no settings configured within Windows

5. What is the difference between ISDN and dial-up?
  A. Both use dialing, but dial-up is based on the WAN and use analog lines, whereas ISDN and DSL are both digital.
  B. Neither use dialing, but dial-up is based on the telephone system and use analog lines, whereas ISDN and DSL are both analog.
  C. Both use dialing, but dial-up is based on the telephone system and use digital lines, whereas ISDN and DSL are both digital.
  D. Both use dialing, but dial-up is based on the telephone system and use analog lines, whereas ISDN and DSL are both digital.

Answers

1. Correct answer and explanation: B. When working with ISDN technology, always remember that the transmission rate of a single BRI ISDN B channel is 64 Kbps.

Incorrect answers and explanations: A, C, and D. Answer A is incorrect because the rate is 64 Kbps, not 56 Mbps. Answer C is incorrect because the rate is 64 Kbps, not 128 Kbps. Answer D is incorrect because the rate is 64 Kbps, not 256 Mbps.

2. Correct answer and explanation: C. ISDN provides better speed, connection time, and reliability compared with a modem. ISDN can be connected to systems in many ways because of the different adapters that can be used with it. ISDN circuits will be terminated on a device or within a location, not on a modem, or on individual workstations using modems.

Incorrect answers and explanations: A, B, and D. Answer A is incorrect because ISDN circuits will be terminated on a device or within a location, not on a modem, or on individual workstations using modems. Answer B is incorrect because ISDN circuits do not terminate on workstations. Answer D is incorrect because ISDN circuits will be terminated on a device or within a location, not on a modem, or on individual workstations using modems.

3. Correct answer and explanation: D. BRI ISDN provides up to 128 Kbps.

Incorrect answers and explanations: A, B, and C. Answer A is incorrect because a T1 is a dedicated connection, it's always on, and you always pay for its use. It's also 1.544 Mbps. Answer B is incorrect because a T3, much like a T1, is a dedicated connection providing up to 45 Mbps. Answer C is incorrect because a 56 Kbps leased line will only provide up to 56 Kbps.

4. Correct answer and explanation: A. If there is no dial tone on the line, you will not be able to dial out to the RAS server to connect to your corporate network. For the Network+ exam, you will be expected to troubleshoot many scenarios; so make sure you read them very carefully.

Incorrect answers and explanations: B, C, and D. Answer B is incorrect because neither the modem nor the PC is the problem; the problem is with the carrier. There is no dial tone and therefore you will not be able to dial out. Answer **C** is incorrect because the modem settings are not the root cause of the problem. Answer **D** is incorrect because the Windows operating system is installed on a PC, which has nothing to do with the absence of dial tone.

5. Correct answer and explanation: **D**. Both use dialing, but dial-up is based on the telephone system and use analog lines, whereas ISDN and DSL are both digital.

   Incorrect answers and explanations: **A**, **B**, and **C**. Answer **A** is incorrect because dial-up is not based on the WAN but rather telephone systems. Answer **B** is incorrect because both use dialing and ISDN and DSL are both digital. Answer **C** is incorrect because dial-up is based on the telephone system and use analog lines.

CHAPTER 8

Security Standards and Services

Exam objectives in this chapter
- Hardware and Software Security Devices
- Security Zones
- Network Ports, Services, and Threats
- Network Access Security

HARDWARE AND SOFTWARE SECURITY DEVICES

Many tools that exist today will allow you to monitor, detect, and contain malicious activity in your environment. Each of these tools assists you in being well armed and well prepared to handle any malicious attacks that might come your way.

Intrusion Detection Systems

An intrusion detection system (IDS) is a specialized tool that attempts to determine when malicious activity is occurring within the network. It can make this determination using a variety of different methods and features:

- Some IDSes read and interpret the contents of log files from sensors placed on the network, routers, firewalls, servers, and other network devices, and attempt to match patterns in the log files.
- Some IDSes monitor all the traffic traversing a network segment and use signatures to match the traffic to known attack patterns.
- Some IDSes are run on a network with a known good baseline of traffic. Once they learn the "safe" traffic patterns, it attempts to determine when abnormal activity is occurring which might be an indication of an attack.
- Any of these IDS types could issue alarms or alerts and take various kinds of automatic action in response to suspected attacks.
- An IDS is designed and used to detect, attacks or unauthorized use of systems, networks, and related resources.

- IDSes may be software-based or may combine hardware and software.
- Network IDS exists for the purpose of catching malicious activity once the activity occurs anywhere within your network environment.

Intrusion Prevention Systems

An intrusion prevention system (IPS) is basically the same tool as an IDS except that it has the capability to take some sort of action in response to a suspected attack, such as blocking the malicious network traffic.

An IPS is capable of responding to attacks when they occur, such as:

- Halting the attack in progress.
- Automatically updating firewall and router rules to block future traffic from the same address.

FIREWALLS

A firewall blocks access to an internal network from outside and blocks users of the internal network from accessing potentially dangerous external networks or ports. There are three distinct firewall technologies:

- **Packet filtering** A network layer firewall or packet-filtering firewall works at the network layer of the Open Systems Interconnection (OSI) model and can be configured to deny or allow access to specific ports or Internet Protocol (IP) addresses. It is designed to operate rapidly by either allowing or denying packets simply based on source and destination IP address and port information. This is the simplest and fastest form of traffic-filtering firewall technologies.
  - It works in two directions: to keep intruders at bay and to restrict access to the external network from internal users.
  - Two distinct firewall base policies are as follows:
    - Allow by default – it allows all traffic to pass through the firewall except traffic that is specifically denied.
    - Deny by default – it blocks all traffic from passing through the firewall except for traffic that is explicitly allowed.
  - Ports 0 through 1023 are considered well-known ports. These ports are used for specific network services and should be considered the only ports allowed to transmit traffic through a firewall.
  - Ports outside the range of 0 through 1023 are either registered ports or dynamic/private ports.
    - User ports range from 1024 to 49,151.
    - Dynamic/private ports range from 49,152 to 65,535.
  - Since only the header of a packet is examined, a packet-filtering firewall has speed.
  - There are two major drawbacks to packet filtering:
    - A port is either open or closed.
    - It does not understand the contents of any packet beyond the header.
- **Stateful inspection** Stateful inspection operates at the network and the transport layers of the OSI model, but it has the ability to monitor

state information regarding a connection. In effect, when a connection is established between two hosts, the firewall will initially determine if the connection is allowable based on a set of rules about source and destination ports and IP addresses. Once the connection is deemed to be acceptable, the firewall remembers this. Therefore, subsequent traffic can be examined as either permissible or not within the context of the entire session. It then functions by checking each packet to verify that it is an expected response to a current communications session.

- **Application-layer gateways** They are also called as application-layer gateway devices or application filtering. Application-layer gateways are more advanced than packet filtering, operate at the application layer of the OSI model, and examine the entire packet to determine what should be done with the packet based on specific defined rules. They use complex rules to determine the validity of any given packet, and part of analyzing each packet includes verifying that it contains the correct type of data for the specific application it is attempting to communicate with.
  - The drawbacks to application-layer gateway technology are as follows:
    - Application-layer gateways are much slower than packet filters.
    - A limited set of application rules are predefined and any application not included in the predefined list must have custom rules defined and loaded into the firewall.
    - Application-layer gateways must then rebuild packets from the top down and send them back out. This breaks the concept behind the client/server architecture and slows the firewall down even further.

Proxy Servers

A proxy server is a server that sits between an intranet and its Internet connection and provides features such as document caching for faster browser retrieval and access control.

- Proxy servers can provide security for a network by filtering and discarding requests that are deemed inappropriate by an administrator.
- Proxy servers protect the internal network by masking all internal IP addresses – all connections to the Internet servers appear to be coming from the IP address of the proxy servers.

Honeypot

A honeypot is a computer system that is deliberately exposed to public access for express purpose of attracting and distracting attackers. The following characteristics are typical of honeypots:

- Systems or devices used as lures are set up with only "out of the box" default installations so that they are deliberately made subject to all known vulnerabilities, exploits, and attacks.
- The systems or devices used as lures do not include sensitive information, so these lures can be compromised, or even destroyed, without causing damage, loss, or harm to the organization that presents them to be attacked.

- Systems or devices used as lures often also contain deliberately tantalizing objects or resources to attract and hold an attacker's interest long enough to give a backtrace a chance of identifying the attack's point of origin.
- Systems or devices used as lures also include or are monitored by passive applications that can detect and report on attacks or intrusions as soon as they start, so the process of backtracing and identification can begin as soon as possible.

Honeynets

A honeynet is a network that is set up to attract potential attackers and distract them from your production network. In a honeynet, attackers will not only find vulnerable services or servers but also find vulnerable routers, firewalls, and other network boundary devices, security applications, and so forth. The following characteristics are typical of honeynets:

- Network devices used as lures are set up with only "out of the box" default installations so that they are deliberately made subject to all known vulnerabilities, exploits, and attacks.
- The devices used as lures do not include sensitive information, so these lures can be compromised, or even destroyed, without causing damage, loss, or harm to the organization that presents them to be attacked.
- Devices used as lures also include or are monitored by passive applications that can detect and report on attacks or intrusions as soon as they start, so the process of backtracing and identification can begin as soon as possible.

Content filtering is the process used by various applications to examine content and make a decision based on the analysis of the content and the resulting actions can result in block or allow.

Protocol analyzer takes a capture of each packet for later analysis, as traffic moves across the network from machine-to-machine. They are called by many names such as *packet analyzer*, *network analyzer*, and *sniffer*. Characteristics of protocol analyzers are as follows:

- Capture data is essentially a photocopy, and the original packet is not harmed or altered.
- All broadcast traffic will be captured.
- To capture traffic addressed to/from another machine on the network, the sniffer should be run in promiscuous mode.
- If a hub exists on the network, this allows the capturing of all packets on the network regardless of their source or destination.

EXAM WARNING

Remember that an IPS is designed to be a preventive control. When an IDS identifies patterns that may indicate suspicious activities or attacks, an IPS can take immediate action that can block traffic, blacklist an IP address, or even segment an infected host to a separate virtual local area network (VLAN) that can only access an antivirus server.

SECURITY ZONES

You must imagine the different pieces that make up a network as discrete network segments, called *security zones*, each holding systems that share common requirements. Characteristics of security zones include the following:

- Systems in a zone may be running different protocols and OSes, such as Windows and NetWare.
- The type of a computer and its operating system do not dictate a particular security zone.
- Where the machine resides in the environment helps to define the security zone it resides in.
- Common requirements of a security zone may include the following:
  - The types of information the zone handles.
  - Who uses the zone.
  - What levels of security the zone requires to protect its data.

EXAM WARNING

A security zone is defined as any portion of a network that has specific security concerns or requirements. Intranets, extranets, demilitarized zones (DMZs), and VLANs are all security zones.

The following are samples of security zones that may be defined in your environment:

- **DMZs** A DMZ is a network segment which exists between the hostile Internet and the trusted internal network. Often, systems which need to be made accessible to the public Internet are placed in the DMZ, which offers some basic levels of protection against attacks but is not considered as secure as the trusted internal network.
  - DMZ segments can exist in one of the following two ways:
    - Layered DMZ implementation – the systems that require protection are placed between two firewall devices with different rule sets, which allow systems on the Internet to connect to the offered services on the DMZ systems, but prevent them from connecting to the computers on the internal segments of the organization's network.
    - Multiple interface firewall implementation – a third interface is added to the firewall and the systems that require protection are placed on that network segment. The same firewall is used to manage the traffic between the Internet, the DMZ, and the protected network. See Figure 8.1 for a diagram of a multiple interface firewall implementation.

The role of the firewall in all these scenarios is to manage the traffic between the network segments. The systems in the DMZ can host any or all the following services:

- **Hypertext Transfer Protocol (HTTP) servers** Internet Information Services (IIS) or Apache servers provide Web sites for public and private usage.

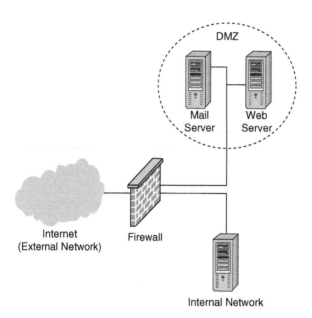

FIGURE 8.1
A multiple interface
firewall DMZ
implementation

- **File Transfer Protocol (FTP) services** FTP file servers provide public and private downloading and uploading of files.

> **EXAM WARNING**
>
> Remember that FTP has significant security issues in which username and password information is passed in clear text and can easily be sniffed.

- **E-mail relaying** E-mail relaying is a special e-mail server that acts as a middleman by accepting messages and passing them through to their destination. E-mail relays are typically disabled on all publicly accessible e-mail servers.
- **Domain name system (DNS) services** A DNS server might be placed in the DMZ to point incoming access requests to the appropriate server within the DMZ. It is important to be careful and ensure that DNS servers in the DMZ cannot be made to conduct a zone transfer to any server.
- **Intrusion detection** IDSes placed in the DMZ will tend to give more false positive results than those inside the private internal network, due to the nature of Internet traffic. To reduce the larger number of false positives, you must perform IDS tuning, which is the process of adjusting the settings on your IDS so that it is more appropriately configured to recognize normal traffic patterns in your environment.

Many organizations choose to implement a multiple segment structure to better manage and secure their different types of business information. The two segments that are widely accepted are as follows:

- A segment dedicated to information storage.
- A segment specifically for the processing of business information.

Each of these two new segments has special security and operability concerns above and beyond those of the rest of the organizational network. Considerations when defining segments are as follows:

- Creation of multiple segments changes a network structure.
- As a site grows and offers new features, new zones may have to be created.
- It is best to start with deny-all strategies and permit only the services and the network transactions required to make the network function.
- Access controls regulate the way network communications are initiated.

EXAM WARNING

A deny-all strategy means that there is a firewall rule which blocks all traffic. Additional rules are created to allow only the minimum level of service required for the network to function. Any traffic that does not match these rules permitting traffic is then handled by the default block rule and the traffic is dropped.

Virtual Private Networks

Virtual private networks (VPNs) allow a remote user to behave as if attached to a local network. The traffic shared among devices on the VPN must be protected so as to provide confidentiality, integrity, and authentication (see Figure 8.2).

Crunch Time

Point-to-Point Tunneling Protocol (PPTP) is a VPN protocol that is a relatively simple encapsulation of the Point-to-Point Protocol (PPP) over an existing Transmission Control Protocol/Internet Protocol (TCP/IP) connection. Characteristics of PPTP include the following:

- Consists of two connections:
  - The control connection is a TCP connection to port 1723.
  - The IP tunnel connection and user data is implemented via PPP in conjunction with the Generic Routing Encapsulation (GRE) protocol.
- PPTP connections can be established in either direction.
- Security requirements of PPTP, such as authentication and encryption, are left to the PPP portion of the traffic.

- PPTP connections can be authenticated through the PPP layer using Microsoft's Challenge Handshake Authentication Protocol (MS-CHAP) or the Extensible Authentication Protocol–Transport Layer Security (EAP–TLS) protocol.
- Encryption can be provided by the Microsoft Point-to-Point Encryption (MPPE) protocol, which is based on RC4 with session keys of 40-bit, 56-bit, or 128-bit length.
- Because of the need for two connections to maintain a single PPTP tunnel, making sure PPTP traffic can traverse firewalls can be problematic. Also, owing to the use of GRE, traffic originating from or sent to a host that sits behind a device performing Network Address Translation (NAT).

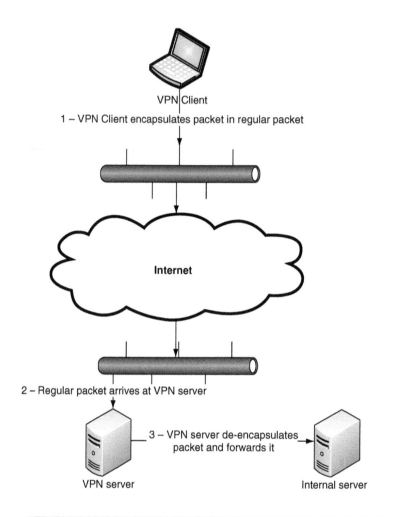

FIGURE 8.2
A VPN in use

Layer 2 Tunneling Protocol (L2TP) is a VPN protocol which is tunneled over User Datagram Protocol (UDP). Characteristics of the L2TP are as follows:

- L2TP uses one data stream only, on UDP port 1701.
- L2TP packets are divided between control and data by a flag in the header.
- L2TP operates over UDP, so it has to implement its own acknowledgment and retransmission mechanisms for the control messages it uses.
- L2TP uses PPP to encapsulate data traffic that is sent across the tunnel and connections, or "calls" are created and torn down over the implied circuit created by the UDP traffic to port 1701 at the server.
- The server responds to whatever port the client sent its UDP messages from – this may be port 1701, but is generally a random port number.
- L2TP's main usability benefit comes in its use of a single pseudoconnection over a protocol that is forwarded by most routers, UDP.
- L2TP's biggest security benefit comes from the use of a well-defined protocol – Internet Protocol Security (IPSec).

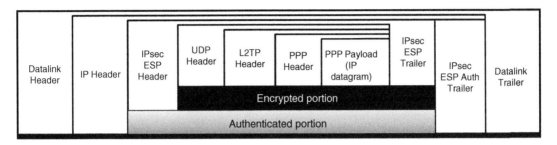

FIGURE 8.3
L2TP/IPSec packet showing multiple levels of encapsulation

- L2TP is most often used as a VPN by combining it with IPSec Encapsulating Security Payload (ESP) so that VPN traffic is encapsulated in five layers (see Figure 8.3) from the outermost layer to the innermost layer:
  1. IP
  2. IPSec ESP
  3. UDP
  4. L2TP
  5. PPP

NETWORK PORTS, SERVICES, AND THREATS

Unnecessary network ports and protocols in your environment should be eliminated whenever possible. By identifying the ports that are open but may not be in use, you will be able to monitor required services and remove all others thereby reducing the opportunity for attack. Many of our internal networks today use TPC/IP as the primary protocol. So, for most that means eliminating the following protocols:

- Internetwork Packet Exchange (IPX)
- Sequenced Packet Exchange (SPX)
- Network Basic Input/Output System (NetBIOS) Extended User Interface (NetBEUI)

It is also important to look at the specific operational protocols used in a network, such as

- Internet Control Messaging Protocol (ICMP)
- Internet Group Management Protocol (IGMP)
- Service Advertising Protocol (SAP)
- Network Basic Input/Output System (NetBIOS)
- Server Message Block (SMB)

Once the network has been secured according to policy, scans should be conducted on a periodic basis to ensure that the network is in compliance with policy. Although there are many different varieties and methods of attack, they can generally all be grouped into several categories:

- By the general target of the attack (application, network, or mixed).
- By whether the attack is active or passive.
- By how the attack works (for example, via password cracking or by exploiting code and cryptographic algorithms).

It's important to realize that the boundaries between these three categories aren't fixed, which has spawned the new term "mixed threat applications." Sample network threats include the following:

- **TCP/IP hijacking** TCP/IP hijacking, or session hijacking, is when a malicious user intercepts a legitimate user's data and then inserts themselves into that session much like a man-in-the-middle attack (MITM). The use of encrypted sessions is critical in prevention.
- **Null sessions** Null sessions are unauthenticated connections. Null sessions present vulnerability in that once someone has successfully connected to a machine there is a lot to be learned about the machine.
- **IP spoofing** Spoofing, by definition, is always intentional. There are different types of IP spoofing attacks. These include *blind spoofing attacks* in which the attacker can only send packets and has to make assumptions or guesses about replies and *informed attacks* in which the attacker can monitor, and therefore participate in, bidirectional communications.
- **MITMs** A TCP/IP connection is formed with a three-way handshake. As seen in Figure 8.4, a host (Host A) that wants to send data to another host (Host B) will initiate communications by sending a synchronization (SYN) packet. The SYN packet contains, among other things, IP address of the source and the destination, as well as the port numbers of the source and the destination. Host B will respond with an, acknowledgment and synchronization (SYN/ACK). The SYN from Host B prompts Host A to send another ACK and the connection is established.

  In an MITM, a malicious individual steps in between the two hosts and passes all traffic between their own systems before forwarding it on. In essence, the attacker is masquerading as Host A when communicating with Host B and as Host B when communicating with Host A. Because all packets between the two hosts pass through the attacker, he can then monitor the packets and capture the entire communication stream between the two hosts. The attacker can even change the packets coming and going to a particular host.
- **Replay attacks** In a replay attack, a malicious person captures an amount of sensitive traffic and then simply replays it back to the host in an attempt to replicate the transaction.

FIGURE 8.4
A standard TCP/IP handshake

- **Denial of Service (DoS)** These attacks attempt to render a network inaccessible by flooding a device, such as a firewall, with packets to the point that it can no longer accept valid packets.
  - **Distributed DoS (DDoS)** An alternative attack that is more difficult to defend against is the DDoS attack, which can come from a large number of computers at the same time.
- **DNS poisoning** DNS poisoning or DNS cache poisoning occurs when a server is fed altered or spoofed records that are then retained in the DNS server cache.
- **Address Resolution Protocol (ARP) poisoning** ARP poisoning occurs when a client machine sends out an ARP request for another machine's Media Access Control (MAC) address information and is sent falsified information instead.

NETWORK ACCESS SECURITY

Authentication, Authorization, and Auditing (AAA) together make up the concept of Network Access Security. AAA is a group of processes used to protect the data, equipment, and confidentiality of property and information. One of the goals of AAA is to provide Confidentiality, Integrity, and Availability (CIA). CIA can be briefly described as follows:

- **Confidentiality** to protect data from unauthorized disclosure.
- **Integrity** to protect data from unauthorized alteration.
- **Availability** to protect data from being destroyed or rendered inaccessible to authorized users.

AAA consists of three separate areas that work together. These areas provide a level of basic security in controlling access to resources and equipment in networks. This control allows users to provide services that assist in the CIA process for further protection of systems and assets.

- **Authentication** Authentication can be defined as the process used to verify that a machine or user attempting access to the networks or resources is, in fact, the entity being presented.
- **Authorization** Authorization can be defined as a policy, software component, or hardware component that is used to grant or deny access to a resource. It can also be a rule set that defines the operation of a software component limiting entrance to a system or network.
- **Auditing** Auditing is the process of tracking and reviewing events, errors, access, and authentication attempts on a system.

Authentication Methods

Authentication is the process used to prove the identity of someone or something that wants access. Only through a trusted and secure method of authentication, administrators can provide for a trusted and secure communication or activity.

ONE-FACTOR

With one-factor authentication, only one form of authenticator is used in conjunction with a username. Often, the single authenticator is a password, or PIN. Password policies come in the following three security levels:

- Low (or no) – six characters long or less.
- Medium – between 8 and 13 characters.
- High – policies requiring 14 or more characters.

Additionally, all password policies, regardless of password length, should require an acceptable password that contains a combination of the following:

- Uppercase and lowercase alphabetic characters
- Numbers
- Special characters
- No dictionary words
- No portion of the username in the password
- No personal identifiers should be used, including birthdays, social security number, pet's name, and so on.

TWO-FACTOR

Two-factor authentication can be implemented by requiring a user to provide an authenticator from two categories of authenticators. To misuse your authentication credentials in a two-factor authentication scheme, an attacker must acquire both.

Token technology is a method that can be used in networks and facilities to authenticate users. The tokens are a physical device used for the randomization of a code that can be used to assure the identity of the individual or service that has control of them.

MULTIFACTOR

Three-factor authentication or commonly known as *multifactor authentication* should use three independent authentication mechanisms available. The following are four possible types of factors that can be used in a multifactor authentication implementation:

- A password or a PIN can be defined as a *something you know* factor.
- A token or Smart Card can be defined as a *something you have* factor.
- A thumbprint, retina, hand, or other biometrically identifiable item can be defined as a *something you are* factor.
- Voice or handwriting analysis can be used as a *something you do* factor.

SINGLE SIGN-ON

Single Sign-On (SSO) is a process in which we simplify the access to different systems by authenticating the user once. Benefits of SSO include direct reduction in password fatigue that users experience by having to logon to and keep track of so many different authentication credentials and simplified management. SSO can be implemented through various network operating systems (NOS) including Microsoft Windows 2003 Internet Authentication Services (IASes), Microsoft Windows 2008 Network Policy Server (NPS), and Linux systems using Kerberos or through non-OS implementations such as RSA Enterprise Single Sign-On (ESSO) solutions.

Authentication Services

Authentication services refer to the directory services accessed before the users are authenticated or services used to authenticate.

REMOTE ACCESS SERVICES

Remote access policies go beyond just authenticating the user. These policies *define* how the users can connect to the network. You may also grant or deny the permission to dial-in, based on the credentials presented by the remote users. A remote access policy defines the conditions, remote access permissions, and creates a profile for every remote connection made to the corporate network.

Through remote access policies you can define the following:

- Grant or deny dial-in based on connection parameters such as type and time of the day
- Authentication protocols (Password Authentication Protocol (PAP), CHAP, EAP, MS-CHAP)
- Validation of the caller id
- Call back
- Apply connection restrictions upon successful authorization
- Create remote user/connection profile
- Assign a static IP or dynamic IP from the address pool defined for remote users
- Assign the user to a group to apply group policies
- Configure remote access permission parameters
- Define encryption parameters (for a remote access VPN client)
- Control the duration of the session including maximum time allowed and the idle time before the connection is reset

Remote access policies can be configured in Microsoft Windows 2003 through IAS, in Windows 2008 through NPS and in Linux variants through Free Remote Authentication Dial-In User Service (RADIUS).

REMOTE AUTHENTICATION DIAL-IN USER SERVICE AND BIOMETRICS

When users dial into a network, RADIUS is used to authenticate usernames and passwords. A RADIUS server can either work alone or in a distributed environment, known as *distributed RADIUS*, where RADIUS servers are configured in a hierarchical structure. RADIUS supports a number of protocols including the following:

- Point-to-Point Protocol (PPP)
- Password Authentication Protocol (PAP)
- Challenge Handshake Authentication Protocol (CHAP.)

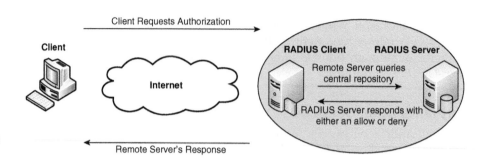

FIGURE 8.5
RADIUS authentication
process

In a distributed RADIUS environment, a RADIUS server forwards the authentication request to an enterprise RADIUS server using a protocol called *proxy RADIUS*. RADIUS may be vulnerable to buffer overflow attacks. The RADIUS authentication process is depicted in Figure 8.5.

Biometric devices can provide a higher level of authentication than, for example, a username/password combination.

KERBEROS

Kerberos is a network protocol designed to centralize the authentication information for the user or service requesting the resource. This allows authentication of the entity requesting access (user, machine, service, or process) by the host of the resource being accessed through the use of secure and encrypted keys and tickets (*authentication tokens*) from the authenticating key distribution center (KDC).

Characteristics of Kerberos are as follows:

- It allows for cross-platform authentication.
- It centralizes the processing of credentials for authentication.
- Kerberos uses time stamping of its tickets to help ensure that they are not compromised by other entities. It uses an overall structure of control that is called a *realm*.
- In a Kerberos realm, the Key Distribution Server (KDC) acts as both an authentication server and as a ticket granting server.
- Kerberos uses a time stamp to limit the possibility of replay or spoofing of credentials. Microsoft's Kerberos implementation has a 5-min. time delta. If clocks are not synchronized between the systems, the credentials (tickets) will not be granted if the time differential exceeds the established limits.

LIGHTWEIGHT DIRECTORY ACCESS PROTOCOL

Directory services are used to store, retrieve, and manage information about objects, such as user accounts, computer accounts, mail accounts, and information on resources available on the network. Some of the directory services that are produced by vendors include the following:

- **Active Directory** was developed by Microsoft for networks running Windows 2000 Server, Windows 2003 Server, or Windows 2008.

- **eDirectory** was developed by Novell for Novell NetWare networks. Previous versions for Novell NetWare 4.x and 5.x were called *Novell Directory Services* (NDS).
- **OpenLDAP** was developed by Apple for networks running Mac OS X Servers.

Lightweight Directory Access Protocol (LDAP) is a protocol that enables clients to access information within a directory service, allowing the directory to be searched and objects to be added, modified, and deleted.

- Characteristics of LDAP are as follows:
  - LDAP was created after the X.500 specification that uses the Directory Access Protocol (DAP).
  - LDAP directories follow a hierarchy using a tree-like structure, where the top of the hierarchy is called the *root*. The root server is used to create the structure of the directory, with organizational units (OU) and the objects branching out from the root.
  - Parts of the directory structure may exist on different servers. Segmenting the tree based on organization or division and storing each branch on separate directory servers increases the security of the LDAP information.
  - The topmost level of the hierarchy generally uses the DNS namespace to identify the tree.
- Characteristics of the OU are as follows:
  - OUs are used to identify different branches of the organization or network.
  - To identify the OUs, each has a name that must be unique in its place in the hierarchy.
  - Each OU can be nested in other OUs.
  - You can't have two OUs with the same name in the same parent OU.
  - You can have OUs with the same name in different areas of the hierarchy.
- Objects and Attributes:
  - The name given to each object is referred to as a common name, which identifies the object but doesn't show where it resides in the hierarchy.
  - You can't have two objects with the same name in an OU.
  - A *distinguished name* is used to identify the object's place in the hierarchy.
  - The distinguished name is a unique identifier for the object and is made up of several attributes of the object. It consists of the *relative distinguished name*, which is constructed from some attribute(s) of the object, followed by the distinguished name of the parent object.
- Schema and Classes:
  - The schema defines the object classes and the attribute types.
  - Object classes define what the object represents (that is, user, computer, and so forth) and a list of what attributes are associated with the object.
  - Each of the attributes associated with an object is defined in the schema.
  - Because LDAP is binary, to view the attributes of an object, the information can be represented in LDAP Data Interchange Format (LDIF).

- Securing LDAP:
  - LDAP clients must authenticate to the server before being allowed access to the directory.
  - The LDAP server constitutes a security realm, which is used to authenticate users.
  - Clients (users, computers, or applications) connect to the LDAP server using a distinguished name and authentication credentials, usually a password.
  - It is possible for users to make the connection with limited or no authentication, by using either anonymous or simple authentication.
  - To secure LDAP, anonymous clients should be limited or not used, ensuring that only those with proper credentials are allowed access to the information.
  - Authentication information is sent from the client to the server as part of a "bind" operation, and the connection is later closed using an "unbind" operation.
  - The connection can be configured to use TLS to secure transmissions and protect any data sent between the client and the server.
  - LDAP can also be used over Secure Sockets Layer (SSL), which encrypts LDAP connections.
  - TCP/UDP port 389 and LDAPS uses port 636.

PASSWORD AUTHENTICATION PROTOCOL AND CHALLENGE HANDSHAKE AUTHENTICATION PROTOCOL

- **PAP** PAP was used to authenticate users using usernames and passwords. PAP uses a two-way handshake and transmits the username and password in American Standard Code for Information Interchange (ASCII) without any encryption. PAP was replaced by CHAP to provide more security.
- **CHAP** CHAP is a remote access authentication protocol used in conjunction with PPP to provide security and authentication to users of remote resources. CHAP is used to periodically verify the identity of the peer using a three-way handshake. This is done upon initial link establishment and may be repeated anytime after the link has been established.

TERMINAL ACCESS CONTROLLER ACCESS CONTROL SYSTEM/TERMINAL ACCESS CONTROLLER ACCESS CONTROL SYSTEM PLUS

Terminal access controller access control system (TACACS) is used in authenticating remote users. TACACS has gone through three major "generations":

- **TACACS** TACACS was first developed during the days of Advanced Research Projects Agency Network (ARPANET), and it offers authentication and authorization, but it does not offer any accounting tools.
- **Terminal Access Controller Access-Control System Plus (TACACS+)** TACACS+ is a Cisco proprietary version of TACACS that is incompatible with previous versions. TACACS+ uses individual databases for each.

TACACS+ was the first revision to offer secure communications between the TACACS+ client and the TACACS+ server. Vulnerabilities and attacks common with TACACS+ are as follows:

- The encryption used in TACACS+ is based on a shared secret that is rarely changed, so a compromise at any point would ultimately expose future compromises.
- **Birthday attacks** The pool of TACACS+ session IDs is not very large; therefore, it is reasonable that two users could have the same session ID.
- **Buffer overflow** Like RADIUS, TACACS+ can fall victim to buffer-overflow attacks.
- **Packet sniffing** The length of passwords can be easily determined by "sniffing" a network.
- **Lack of integrity checking** An attacker can alter accounting records during transmission because the accounting data is not encrypted during transport.

EXAM WARNING

Make sure you understand the difference between TACACS and TACACS+. The most important thing to remember is that TACACS uses UDP as its transport protocol, whereas TACACS+ uses TCP. Also, TACACS+ is a proprietary version owned by Cisco.

MUTUAL AUTHENTICATION

Mutual authentication is a process where both the requestor and the target entity must fully identify themselves before communication or access is allowed.

DID YOU KNOW?

Characteristics of mutual authentication are as follows:

- You can share a secret or you can use a Diffie-Hellman key exchange or certificates.
- To verify the identities, the Certificate Authority (CA) must be known to both parties, and the public keys for both must be available from the trusted CA.
- The mutual authentication process is used for access of a user to a network via remote access or authentication via a RADIUS server.
- 802.1X and EAP provide for a mutual authentication capability.
- Mutual authentication assists in the mitigation of attacks from MITM types of devices.
- Any of the following EAP methods provide for mutual authentication:
  - **TLS** requires that the server supply a certificate and establish that it has possession of the private key.
  - **Internet Key Exchange (IKE)** requires that the server show possession of a preshared key or private key (this can be considered certificate authentication).
  - **GSS_API (Kerberos)** requires that the server can demonstrate knowledge of the session key.

- Institute of Electrical and Electronics Engineers, Inc. (IEEE) 802.11w
  - The IEEE 802.11b standard is only for the open and shared-key authentication scheme, which is nonextensible.
  - The IEEE 802.11w is a proposed amendment to the existing 802.11 standards to increase security.
  - The 802.11w defines enhancements for integrity, authenticity and confidentiality of the data, and ensure protection from replay attacks.

EXTENSIBLE AUTHENTICATION PROTOCOL

EAP is an authentication protocol designed to support several different authentication mechanisms. It runs directly over the data link layer and does not require the use of IP.

EAP comes in several different forms:

- EAP over IP (EAPoIP)
- Message Digest Algorithm/Challenge Handshake Authentication Protocol (EAP-MD5-CHAP)
- EAP–TLS
- EAP–Tunneled Transport Layer Security (TTLS)
- RADIUS
- Cisco EAP-Flexible Authentication via Secure Tunneling (FAST)

EAP can support per-packet authentication and integrity protection, but it is not extended to all types of EAP messages. For example, negative acknowledgment (NACK) and notification messages cannot use per-packet authentication and integrity. Per-packet authentication and integrity protection works for the following (packet is encrypted unless otherwise noted):

- TLS and IKE derive session key
- TLS ciphersuite negotiations (not encrypted)
- IKE ciphersuite negotiations
- Kerberos tickets
- Success and failure messages that use a derived session key (through Wireless Encryption Protocol (WEP))

PROTECTED EXTENSIBLE AUTHENTICATION PROTOCOL

Protected Extensible Authentication Protocol (PEAP) uses TLS to create an encrypted channel between the client supplicant and the RADIUS server.

Security and ease of deployment make PEAP a popular choice for authentication. The advantages of PEAP are as follows:

- Windows 2008, Windows Server 2003, Windows 2000, Windows XP, and Pocket PC 2002 offer support for PEAP (either natively or with a system update), so there is no need for you to install third-party client software.
- NPS in Windows 2008 and IAS in Windows 2003 are the Microsoft implementation of the RADIUS protocol. Windows 2000 Server and Windows

Server 2003 support PEAP, so there is no need to install third-party RADIUS software.

- PEAP uses a TLS channel to protect the user credentials.
- Using the TLS channel from the client to the authentication server, PEAP offers end-to-end protection, not just over the wireless data link.
- PEAP supports any EAP compatible methods.
- PEAP offers strong protection against the deployment of unauthorized wireless application processes (APs) because the client verifies the RADIUS server's identity before proceeding ahead with further authentication or connectivity. The wireless AP is unable to decrypt the authentication messages protected by PEAP.
- PEAP offers highly secure keys that are used to encrypt the data communications between the clients and wireless AP. New encryption keys are derived for each connection and are shared with authorized wireless APs accepting the connection. Unauthorized wireless APs are not provided with the encryption keys.
- PEAP does not require the deployment of certificates to wireless clients. Only the PEAP server (authentication server) needs to be assigned a certificate.
- PEAP is an open standard supported under the security framework of the IEEE 802.1X specification.
- PEAP provides support for EAP authentication methods, such as EAP–TLS and EAP-MS-CHAPV2, that can perform computer authentication.

Summary of Exam Objectives

In today's networking world, networks no longer have to be designed in the same manner. There are many options available as to how to physically and logically design a network. All these above-mentioned options can be used to increase the security of the internal network by keeping the untrusted and the unauthorized users out. The usage of DMZs to segment traffic into a protected zone between external and internal firewalls helps prevent attacks against your Internet facing servers.

VPNs are used to allow remote network users to securely connect back to the corporate network. To additionally reduce the risk in your environment, application and service hardening should be considered. Be familiar with the required ports for various services so that you can uninstall or disable unused services, which will reduce unnecessary exposure. Include evaluation of network services, such as DNS and Dynamic Host Configuration Protocol (DHCP), and specific types of application services, such as e-mail, databases, Network News Transfer Protocol (NNTP) servers, and others.

IDSes are used to identify and respond to attacks on the network. Several types of IDSes exist, each with its own unique pros and cons. An IPS is a newer type of IDS that can quickly respond to perceived attacks. Honeypots and honeynets can be used to distract attackers from real servers and keep them occupied while you collect information on the attack and the source of the attack.

After an attack has occurred, the most important thing to do is to collect all the evidence of the attack and its methods. You will also want to take steps to ensure that the same type of attack cannot be successfully performed on the network in the future. Authentication protocols are chosen based on the applications, complexity, and level of security needs. Kerberos provides access through secure encrypted keys and issuance of tickets. CHAP validates the identity of the clients through three-way handshake (challenge, response, success, or failure).

RADIUS is the most popular of all the AAA servers, which include RADIUS, TACACS, and TACACS+. We also reviewed Extension Authentication Protocol and Protected EAP.

Top Five Toughest Questions

1. You are performing a security audit for a company to determine their risk from various attack methods. As part of your audit, you work with one of the company's employees to see what activities he performs during the day that could be at risk. As you work with the employee, you see him perform the following activities:

   Log into the corporate network using Kerberos
   Access files on a remote system through a Web browser using SSL
   Log into a remote UNIX system using Secure Shell (SSH)
   Connect to a Post Office Protocol 3 (POP3) server and retrieve e-mail
   Which of these activities is most vulnerable to a sniffing attack?
   A. Logging into the corporate network using Kerberos
   B. Accessing files on a remote system through a Web browser using SSL
   C. Logging into a remote UNIX system using SSH
   D. Connecting to a POP3 server and retrieving e-mail

2. You are a security consultant for a large company that wants to make its intranet available to its employees via the Internet. They want to ensure that the site is as secure as possible. To do this, they want to use multifactor authentication. The site uses an ID and password already but they want to add security features that ensure that the site is indeed their site, not a spoofed site, and that the user is an authorized user. Which authentication technology supports this?
   A. Certificates
   B. CHAP
   C. Kerberos
   D. Tokens

3. You have been asked to help a company implement multifactor authentication. They want to make sure that the environment is as secure as possible through the use of biometrics. Based on your knowledge of authentication, you understand that biometrics falls under the "something you are"

category. Which other category should be used with the biometric device to provide the highest level of security?

A. Something you know

B. Something you have

C. Something you do

D. All these options have their own benefits and detriments.

4. When using LDAP for authentication in an internetworking environment, what is the best way to ensure that the authentication data is secure from packet sniffing?

A. Use LDAP to keep all passwords encrypted when transmitted to the server.

B. Use LDAP over SSL/TLS to encrypt the authentication data.

C. Require that the clients use strong passwords so that they cannot easily be guessed.

D. Use LDAP over HTTP/S to encrypt the authentication data.

5. You have been asked to use an existing router and utilize it as a firewall. Management would like you to use it to perform address translation and block some known bad IP addresses that previous attacks have originated from. With this in mind, which of the following statements are accurate?

A. You have been asked to perform NAT services

B. You have been asked to set up a proxy

C. You have been asked to set up stateful inspection

D. You have been asked to set up a packet filter

Answers

1. Correct answer and explanation: **D.** Connecting to a POP3 server sends the ID and password over the network in a nonencrypted format due to the use of clear text authentication. This data (in addition to the e-mail content itself) is consequently vulnerable to being collected when sniffing the network.

   Incorrect answers and explanations: **A, B,** and **C.** Answer **A** is incorrect because logging into a network using Kerberos is secure from sniffing attacks due to encryption and time stamps. Answer **B** is incorrect because using SSL encrypts the connection so that it cannot be viewed by sniffing. Answer **C** is incorrect because using SSH encrypts the connection to the remote UNIX system.

2. Correct answer and explanation: **A.** Certificates can be used not only to ensure that the site is the company's Web site, but also that the user is an authorized user. The Web server can be configured to require client-side certificates.

   Incorrect answers and explanations: **B, C,** and **D.** Answer **B** is incorrect because CHAP does not support two-way authentication in this manner. Answer **C** is incorrect because Kerberos can authenticate the user in a method similar to this, but could not serve to authenticate the server. Answer **D** is incorrect because tokens are used for one-way authentication.

3. Correct answer and explanation: **D**. All these options have their own benefits and detriments. A combination of all of them in a multifactor authentication system would provide the highest level of security although it would be quite an inconvenience to the user.

   Incorrect answers and explanations: Answer **A** is incorrect because, while this is a valid solution for the multifactor authentication requirement, it is not the most secure solution. Answer **B** is incorrect because this too is not the most secure solution. Answer **C** is incorrect as well because any two-factor authentication method is not as secure as a *four-factor authentication* method.

4. Correct answer and explanation: **B**. Use LDAP over SSL/TLS to encrypt the authentication data. This will ensure that no LDAP authentication is performed unencrypted so that anyone capturing the packets on the network will be able to read it easily.

   Incorrect answers and explanations: Answer **A** is incorrect because LDAP doesn't encrypt data transmitted between the client and the server. Answer **C** is incorrect because even though it is important to use strong passwords, it does not protect the authentication data from being captured by a packet sniffer. Answer **D** is incorrect because HTTP/S is a protocol for transferring Web pages securely.

5. Correct answer and explanation: **D**. Answer **D** is correct because a packet filter will evaluate each packet and either block or allow the traffic from reaching its destination based on the rules defined. In this case, the packet filter would examine the packets for the bad IP addresses and the action taken on the packets would be to drop or block them.

   Incorrect answers and explanations: **A**, **B**, and **C**. Answer **A** is incorrect because NAT is the process of mapping external to internal IP addresses, which is not being described here. Answer **B** is incorrect because a proxy server functions as a middle device which passes information from a requesting client to a destination server, and then, once a response is received from the server back to the proxy, the proxy passes the information back to the requesting client. Proxy servers can be used to speed up responses by caching content such as Web pages, and they can also be used for security purposes to keep the internal clients hidden from the external world. Answer **C** is incorrect because stateful inspection is when a device, typically a firewall, keeps track of state of network connections. This allows the firewall to detect when packets have been modified or if they are not appropriate to be transmitted, but by only analyzing the header information, the firewall remains efficient.

CHAPTER 9
Network Management

Exam objectives in this chapter
- Network Management
- Configuration Management
- Network Monitoring

NETWORK MANAGEMENT

A common way of characterizing network management functions is by using the acronym FCAPS: fault, configuration, accounting, performance, and security.

Network management can include many functions; some of these functions include planning, allocating, deploying, monitoring resources, load balancing, security management, performance management, bandwidth management, and route analytics.

CONFIGURATION MANAGEMENT

Configuration management (CM) is a practice that involves documentation of a device's configuration, as well as keeping that documentation up-to-date, so that any future changes can be controlled and tracked. By having this information, you can replace devices and make changes to the network quickly.

Fast Facts

The following are some key points related to CM:

- Compile information on the components of your network and create an inventory that can be used to track items that need to be replaced or upgraded.

- Follow a life cycle for computer equipment and replace older machines every 3 or 4 years.

- Network devices, like routers and switches, also need a replacement schedule.

- Keeping a database allows you to schedule upgrades and replacements more easily.

- Managing software and hardware in this fashion also provides a record of computer assets, which can be useful for budgeting hardware refreshes and determining insurance needs.

- If a disaster occurs, the configuration documentation would be used to recreate the configuration of the damaged devices on the new equipment.

CM Documentation Types

CM documentation includes writing schematics, developing physical and logical network diagrams, establishing baselines, creating policy and procedures documents, and documenting configurations and regulations.

So what should be documented? The answer varies across different enterprises, but some considerations include the following:

- **Physical access methods** How does your network physically connect from one office to another? Think about the transmission methods and the speeds that they operate. Consider the standards in use and the cabling types: Ethernet, Token Ring, Unshielded Twisted Pair, Shielded Twisted Pair, Thinnet, and so forth.
- **Service protocols** What protocols do you use on your servers, workstations, data centers, routers, switches, and even your network printers?
- **Hardware devices** How many routers, switches, hubs, rack-mounted servers, workstations, laptops, personal data assistants (PDA), thumb drives, power supplies, printers, networked digital pictures frames, wireless flat screens, bluetooth-enabled devices, and any other wireless devices are on your network right now? How many of each device do you have? Document where they are physically located, vendor service tags, serial numbers, and any other pertinent information.
- **Software applications** What applications are installed on your hardware devices (workstations, servers, routers, switches, firewalls, and printers)? What applications communicate between your clients and servers? How do your applications run? How often does the software vendor release patches, upgrades, and security alerts? Document the current version of your applications.

Documenting Configurations

CM starts by performing an inventory of network components and documenting information about each device. How much data you compile is subjective, but you should include as many specifics as possible. Information included in a database or series of documents may include the following:

- The device asset number
- The name of the device
- The Internet Protocol (IP) address
- The Media Access Control address
- The make, model, and model number
- The serial number and product ID
- The location of the device
- The person who has been issued the device
- The purchase date
- The warranty information and details
- The operating system and service pack information
- Amount of physical memory installed
- The number of processors and their type and speed
- The number of hard disks and their size, type, and speed
- Software information

There are a number of methods and tools available to help you acquire most of the information to be included in your database, but other information can be acquired using various configuration utilities. These tools include but are not limited to ipconfig, ifconfig, winipcfg, and ping.

Change Control Documentation

One of the benefits of compiling information about devices on your network is that it can allow you to see those devices which will be affected by a network change. Change control documentation provides a record of changes that have been made to a system, which can be used in troubleshooting problems and upgrading systems.

DID YOU KNOW?

When you are creating a change control document, at a minimum you should document the following:

1. Describing the change to be made
2. Explaining why this change is required
3. Outlining how the change is to be implemented and detailing the steps to be performed
4. Documenting a rollback strategy

The procedures you document are a valuable resource when you are recovering from a disaster and/or need to install another device or software in the same manner.

Wiring Schematics

- Wiring schematics are simple sketches that are created before and during the installation of the physical media used for computers to talk to each other.
- The physical media used to connect your network are common items to be included when creating wiring schematics.
- When troubleshooting a network connection problem, remember your wiring schematics.

Physical Network Diagrams

- Physical network diagrams contain each physical device and physical connection inside your network.
- Clear and simple physical diagrams go a long way.
- Depending on your network size and complexity, you might need the assistance of network diagram software like Microsoft Visio, SmartDraw, and/or AutoCAD.

Physically laying out your network devices will help you conserve time and money when you need to troubleshoot network issues.

Logical Network Diagrams

- Logical network diagrams depict how your network looks from a configurations perspective, not from the physical layout of the equipment.
- Protocols, configurations, IP addressing, subnets, access control lists, security devices (firewalls, virtual private networks, and so forth), and applications are all logically associated with a computer network and are drawn into logical network diagrams.

Baselines

- A "normal" pattern of behavior is referred to as a baseline.
- Create a baseline and continue to do analysis on this baseline.
- Choosing a baseline method can depend on the size of the network and number of users.
- Many baseline tools collect and monitor activity environmental components, such as the network, specified central processing units, memory, hard drives, and identified network interface cards.

Policies, Procedures, and Configurations

- Policies provide guidelines on who can perform certain actions in the environment.
- Procedures lay out each step needed to accomplish a task.
- Configurations represent the functional specification with which systems in the environment operate on.

DID YOU KNOW?

Policies can be as simple or as complex as the needs of the organization. When creating policies, consider some of the following categories and ask if these need to be addressed in the organization:

- End-User License Agreement
- Network access and user accounts
- Proper destruction of network devices (that is, desktops, servers, and printers)
- Creating administrative and user passwords
- Periodic backups for servers and clients
- Termination of user account access
- Third-party software authorization
- User account lockout and account disabling
- Missing or corrupt computer files
- Malicious code discovery by users
- Natural disaster affecting the network connectivity
- Software management and storage
- IP addressing scheme for contractors
- Computer naming convention for servers
- Network sharing programs for users
- Wide area network (WAN) troubleshooting techniques
- Federal and State computer fraud hot line

Regulations

Regulations guide how to plan and establish policies and procedures. Many organizations are held to state and federal regulations, which will affect their responsibilities as a public/private, for profit or nonprofit business.

Samples of enforceable regulations that may impact different organizations are as follows:

- Health Insurance Portability and Accountability Act (HIPAA)
- Sarbanes-Oxley Act of 2002
- ISO/IEC 27002:2005

NETWORK MONITORING

- **Packet sniffer** This tool allows you to collect all the data that is being transmitted to and from the endpoints on the network. The advantage of collecting individual packets is that you will have an insight and detailed inspection of how certain traffic is being transmitted.
- **Event logs** Logs are records of events that have occurred and actions that were taken. Many systems will provide logs that will give automated information on events that have occurred, including accounts that were used to log on, activities performed by users and by the system, and problems that transpired. On many systems, the logs may be simple text files that are saved

to a location on the local hard drive or a network server. In other cases, the system will provide a specific tool for viewing the information.

- **Password lists** Password lists should contain all the passwords used to perform administrative or maintenance tasks on the network. This includes passwords for
  - Administrative and administrator account for servers and workstations.
  - Setup and configuration utilities on computers and other devices.
  - Administrative features in software.
  - Files, such as those containing other passwords or documentation containing procedures.
- **Notification documentation** Notification documentation includes contact information for specific people in an organization, their roles, and when they should be called. The contact information included in notification documentation should provide several methods of contacting the appropriate person. Notification procedures should also include contact information for certain outside parties who are contracted to support specific systems.

Network Performance Optimization

Network performance optimization is the process of assessing the network's status on an ongoing basis by monitoring and discovering network traffic and logs. Possible monitoring targets include the following: data rates, available bandwidth, WAN link status, backup time, device response rate, and component failures. The methods in which we will use to discover performance issues may include the following:

Crunch Time

Quality of Service (QoS) is a measure of value of a network service compared with the expected or the predicted performance quality that network service is actually producing on your network.

QoS can assist in mitigating issues, such as

- **Dropped packets** – Some, none, or all of the packets might be dropped, depending on the state of the network, and it is impossible to determine what will happen in advance.
- **Delay/Latency** – Overcrowded data links on routers in the transit path of your packets could result in a delay of data packets. Long queues or indirect route avoiding congestion might be some causes of latency within your network.
- **Jitter** – When there are delays in transit, some packets leaving after others might arrive at the destination first. This variation in packet delay is called

"jitter." Applications like Voice over IP (VoIP) cannot be used effectively if *jitter* is excessive.

- **Errors** – Sometimes packets are misdirected, or combined together, or corrupted, while en route.

QoS protocols include the following:

- **Resource Reservation Protocol**
- **Multiprotocol label switching**

QoS models include the following:

- **Differentiated services (DiffServ)** specifies a way of classifying and managing network traffic on IP networks.
- **Integrated services (IntServ)** allows applications to signal associated QoS requirements to the local network before transmitting information.

There are eight levels of QoS as described in Table 9.1.

Table 9.1	Levels of Quality of Service (QoS)
Priority Level	**Traffic Type**
0	Best effort
1	Background
2	Standard (spare)
3	Excellent load (business critical)
4	Controlled load (streaming multimedia)
5	Voice and video (interactive media and voice) [Fewer than 100 ms latency and jitter]
6	Layer 3 network control reserved traffic (Fewer than 10 ms latency and jitter)
7	Layer 2 network control reserved traffic (Lowest latency and jitter)

- **Packet shaping** This technique is used by specifying what traffic at what rate (rate limiting) in a span of time (bandwidth throttling) you are going to allow in or out of your network.
  - *Traffic shaping* is more common at the border routers of an environment working to delay traffic where appropriate as it enters the network.
  - Internal routers and outbound traffic can also be shaped.
  - *Traffic policing* and *traffic contract* are terms used to describe how packets are allowed in/out of the network and at what time.
  - Enforcing compliance with the traffic contract is how traffic sources are aware of what traffic policy is in effect.
  - Traffic shaping shapes the traffic into optimal network utilization for the allocated bandwidth on a particular link.
- **Load balancing** *Load balancing* is a technique used on computer networks to distribute the incoming traffic upon other network devices if there are indications of increased network traffic or "load."
  - Load balancing allows a group or cluster of data center servers to share the inbound traffic all the while seeming as if there actually is only one external connection.
  - Once traffic enters the network via the one external entry point, it is distributed among other servers internally connected to share the high traffic volumes.
- **High availability** *High availability* is a system design protocol, which once implemented assures a specific degree of uptime continuity in a specific period of time.
  - The goal of high availability is to ensure users have the maximum uptime so they can access network resources anytime and anywhere.

- Reducing unplanned downtime increases a business's potential productivity.
- **Caching engines** *Cache* is data that is copied from the original data and is saved for computers to access locally instead of having to retrieve the same data again from the source server.
  - Accessing cached data is quicker since it is stored in a temporary location for a specific amount of time.
  - Cache engines are servers that are dedicated to caching data for clients.
  - If an item in cache is not used often enough, it is discarded until the client requests it again.
  - Common implementations of cache engines will target Web server content.
- **Fault tolerance** Fault tolerance allows continued operations in the event of a system or system component failure.

Summary

In this chapter, we discussed why networked information systems need to be managed. If our goal in network management is to manage our networks so that they don't spiral out of control, we need to always remember the activities, techniques, measures, and gear that pertain to how we operate, administer, maintain, and condition networked information systems.

In this chapter, we covered three main exam objectives: network management, CM, and network monitoring. In the network management section, we discussed how to keep track of resources in the network. In the CM section, we discussed why and how to establish documentation, how baselines can assist in network troubleshooting, and why creating and implementing policies and regulations are important. Finally, we addressed network monitoring, which included a brief example of a few tools and how to use them to conduct network monitoring. While discussing network monitoring, we studied on a few terms like QoS, traffic shaping, load balancing, high availability, and fault tolerance. Each of these terms are very important in the network monitoring construct because each one is directly related to all the rest in assisting with troubleshooting and network optimization.

Top Five Toughest Questions

1. You have just been hired by Aplura Inc., a global Internet service provider (ISP), as their first junior network analyst. Bob, your supervisor was late this morning, and before he picked up his daily cup of coffee he asks you to begin troubleshooting the connectivity from your offices' border router to the border router in your remote office in Sydney, Australia. You find the CM documentation but you are looking for the link speed of your router to determine if it is correct. What piece of information is missing from this document?
   A. Physical access methods
   B. Service protocols

    C. Hardware devices

    D. Software applications

2. As the network manager for a small ISP in Maryland serving more than 2000 customers across the eastern United States, you are in charge of daily operations. Your regional supervisor just received a phone call from Corporate. He asks you over the phone to develop a calculated plan of action to guide decisions and achieve sound outcomes that provide guidelines that the installation contractors will use on how to access the closest data center which will be the location that is outfitted with the latest load balancing technology. What kind of document is your regional supervisor asking you to create?

    A. Common management documentation

    B. CM documentation

    C. Procedure

    D. Policy

3. You want to control and optimize the network traffic entering your domain. What technique will assist your boss in increasing the usable bandwidth and lowering the latency?

    A. Traffic shaping

    B. Load balancing

    C. High availability

    D. Jitter

4. You're VoIP phone rings. You pick it up and say, "Hello?" You listen very closely, but all you can hear is broken speech as if someone is talking very slowly but the words are not coming out right. You notice your VoIP switch is blinking red and you open up a command console to your VoIP switch to see why. Looks like there is a problem with your switch and it is not prioritizing your VoIP traffic above all else. What kind of service do you need to enable to ensure VoIP has the highest priority to ensure your VoIP packets are sent and received first?

    A. QoS

    B. Dropped

    C. Delay

    D. Jitter

5. You are working for Google as an intern for the summer. You have always wondered how googling occurred on the back end of all those servers. You ask your supervisor what technique they use to distribute incoming traffic onto other servers when the traffic load became overbearing for one single server. What technique does your supervisor tell you that Google uses to allow for a group of computers in a cluster to share traffic load?

    A. Traffic shaping

    B. Load balancing

    C. High availability

    D. Packet shaping

Answers

1. Correct answer and explanation: **A**. Answer **A** is correct. How does your network physically connect from one office to another? Are you sharing a Token Ring (802.5) fiber network, WiMAX (802.16) across the boulevard? These are the types of questions you will ask yourself to collect information on physical access methods so you can understand your network configuration in case you need to troubleshoot physical network access errors.

Incorrect answers and explanations: **B**, **C**, and **D**. Answer **B** is incorrect because there is no physical access method information collected under this category. What protocols do you use on your servers, workstations, data centers, routers, switches, and even your network printers? Some printers host configuration Web portals to allow administrators to remotely administer link status and paper jams. Knowing what kind of service protocols are on your network and documenting them will help you determine what you need and what you can get rid of. Answer **C** is incorrect because there is no physical access method information collected. Only hardware device information, such as how many routers, switches, hubs, rack-mounted servers, workstations, laptops, PDAs, thumb drives, power supplies, printers, networked digital pictures frames, wireless flat screens, bluetooth-enabled devices, you have on or off of your network at any given time. Now that you know how many of each device you have, do you know where they are physically located at any given point in time? Do you have the vendor service tags, serial numbers, and contact information mapped to each associated device so you can effectively respond to trouble tickets? This is a great CM piece to have documented because you will always find that you need to locate some piece of equipment that needs repairing. Answer **D** is incorrect because the information you collect for this category is legacy, third-party and proprietary software applications. If you aren't in control of your software and the associated updates you will be playing catch up, and that's no fun. What applications are installed on your hardware devices (workstations, servers, routers, switches, firewalls, and printers)? What applications communicate between your clients and servers? Do you store all of your software in one central repository? How do your applications run? Are they server-based or client-based? How often does the software vendor release patches, upgrades, and security alerts? Do you know the current version of your applications? Asking these questions and documenting the responses can help you answer this type of question, "Are your routers Internetwork Operating System (IOS) compatible with the upcoming network switch upgrade?

2. Correct answer and explanation: **D**. Answer **D** is correct because it provides guidelines on how to address certain subjects. Procedures are much more than guidelines. Procedures lay out each step needed to accomplish a task. For example, when creating a user account, the user ID may be the person's last name and first initial not to exceed eight characters. Detailed steps with procedures help execute policies.

Incorrect answers and explanations: **A, B,** and **C.** Answer **A** is incorrect because this term does not exist in network management. Answer **B** is incorrect because CM documentation is the overall term used to describe writing schematics, developing physical and logical network diagrams, establishing baselines, creating policy, procedures, and configurations, and using regulations. Answer **C** is correct because this document lays out each step needed to accomplish a task.

3. Correct answer and explanation: **A.** Answer **A** is correct because this is a common term used to describe the control of computer network traffic to optimize for peak performance, also known as *packet shaping.* Increasing usable bandwidth and lowering latency are the goals of traffic shaping. This technique is used by specifying what traffic, at what rate (rate limiting) in a span of time (bandwidth throttling) you are going to allow in or out of your network.

Incorrect answers and explanations: **B, C,** and **D.** Answer **B** is incorrect because this is a technique used on computer networks to distribute the incoming traffic upon other network devices if there are indications of increased network traffic or "load." Answer **C** is incorrect because high availability is a system design protocol, which once implemented assures a specific degree of uptime continuity in a specific period of time. The goal of high availability is to ensure users have the maximum uptime so they can access network resources anytime and anywhere. Answer **D** is incorrect because jitter is the variation in packet delay when there are delays in transit.

4. Correct answer and explanation: **A.** Answer **A** is correct because QoS is a measure of value of a network service (that is, VoIP) compared with the expected or the predicted performance quality that network service is actually producing on your network. By enabling QoS for VoIP, you can ensure that voice echoing in the background or other delays are not occurring.

Incorrect answers and explanations: **B, C,** and **D.** Dropped, delay, and jitter are incorrect because each of these problems occurs if QoS is not used. Answer **B** is incorrect because the routers might fail to deliver (drop) some packets if they arrive when their buffers are already full. Some, none, or all of the packets might be dropped, depending on the state of the network, and it is impossible to determine what will happen in advance. The receiving application may ask for this information to be retransmitted, possibly causing severe delays in the overall transmission. Answer **C** is incorrect because VoIP is a real-time application of voice services, any delay would reduce the transmission thereby making it impossible to understand the other person on the distant end. Overcrowded data links on routers in the transit path of your packets could result in a delay of data packets.

Long queues or indirect routes avoiding congestion might be some causes of latency within your VoIP network. Answer **D** is incorrect because the Internet is a complex mesh of interconnected routers connected across the world. There is no single path to a given destination. In fact, some packets travel in completely different paths and end up at the same destination. When there are delays in transit, some packets leaving after others might arrive at the destination first. This variation in packet delay is called "jitter." Applications like VoIP cannot effectively be used if jitter is occurring.

5. Correct answer and explanation: **B**. Answer **B** is correct because load balancing is a technique used on computer networks to distribute the incoming traffic upon other network devices if there are indications of increased network traffic or "load." Load balancing allows a group or cluster of data center servers to share the inbound traffic all the while seeming as if there actually is only one external connection to the Internet. In a typical network configured for load balancing, once traffic comes into the network via the one external entry point, it is distributed among other servers internally connected to share the high traffic volumes.

Incorrect answers and explanation: **A**, **C**, and **D**. Traffic shaping, high availability, and packet shaping do not distribute incoming network traffic to other computer devices. Another common term used to describe the control of computer network traffic to optimize for peak performance is packet shaping. Increasing usable bandwidth and lowering latency are the goals of traffic shaping. This technique is used by specifying what traffic at what rate (rate limiting) in a span of time (bandwidth throttling) you are going to allow in or out of your network. More common is the use of traffic shaping at the border routers (those bordering your network's perimeter) for delaying entering network traffic. High availability is a system design protocol, which once implemented assures a specific degree of uptime continuity in a specific period of time. The goal of high availability is to ensure that users have the maximum uptime, so they can access network resources anytime and anywhere.

CHAPTER 10
Network Troubleshooting

Exam objectives in this chapter
- A Troubleshooting Methodology
- The OSI Model
- Windows Tools
- Linux Tools
- NetWare Troubleshooting
- Other Network Troubleshooting Tools
- Importance of Network Documentation
- How to Use the OSI Model in Troubleshooting
- Troubleshooting the Physical Layer
- Troubleshooting the Data Link Layer
- Troubleshooting the Network Layer
- Troubleshooting the Transport Layer
- Troubleshooting the Session Layer
- Troubleshooting the Presentation Layer
- Troubleshooting the Application Layer

A TROUBLESHOOTING METHODOLOGY

One of the key factors in network troubleshooting is isolating the issue to figure out whether it's being caused by a single workstation or cable, or if it's a larger issue affecting numerous users on your network.

You can break down the troubleshooting process into two major components:

- Gathering information
- Analyzing the information you've gathered

Your first step should be to gather information from your users about the nature of the problem, which can be used to determine which component of the network has failed or is misconfigured.

Some questions you'll probably want to ask include the following:

1. What is the exact nature of the problem? Try to be as specific as possible, and ask follow up questions to gather as many details as possible.
2. How many computers are affected by this problem? If the issue is isolated to a single computer, it is likely that the cause of the problem will be related to the computer itself. If it is affecting all computers on a particular subnet or those connected to a particular hub or switch, you can use this information to help you in the troubleshooting process.
3. When did the problem begin to occur? More specifically, you should find out what changed on the network when the issues first began.

Analyzing and Responding to a Problem

To analyze all of the data to determine the cause of the problem, you should examine each of the following layers in the open system interconnection (OSI) model:

- Layer 1 – Check your physical connectivity, like cables, patch panels, wall jacks, and hubs.
- Layer 2 – Verify that any switches or switch ports are configured and appear to be operating properly.
- Layer 3 – Verify that your routers are configured and functioning properly.
- Layer 4 and above – Check the actual application itself.

To assess the situation at each layer, you need to determine the proper troubleshooting tools to use at each layer. For layer 1, it is often useful to start with simple physical inspections looking for issues with the naked eye. However, fluke meters and other tools can be used to check if wiring is correct or if it has degraded. For layers 2 and above, start with basic connectivity tools like ping, moving on to other tools once you've determined that basic connectivity is in place. Network discovery will help you to document the devices on your network and how they are configured. It is strongly recommended to invest in a network discovery tool; the amount of time it will save you in troubleshooting network connectivity issues will often pay for the cost of the tool.

THE OSI MODEL

You can use your understanding of the OSI model to improve your troubleshooting techniques. When it comes to network troubleshooting, the most important layers of the model are the physical, data link, network, and transport layers.

- **The physical layer** It is the lowest layer of the OSI model, and it involves the actual electrical signals that are going from the network cables into the network interface card (NIC) of a computer, switch, router, or hub. A failure at the hardware level will usually involve the physical components of a computer or device. The physical layer is responsible for a number of functions, which are as follows:

- The type of signal transmission used
- The cable type
- The actual layout or path of the network wiring
- The voltage and electrical signals being used by the network cabling
- The following physical devices function at the physical layer of the OSI model: network cabling, network interface cards, active and passive hubs, and repeaters.
- **The data link layer** The data link layer is responsible for taking the information from the physical layer and organizing it into frames. The functions of the data link layer include the following:
  - Error checking and error-free delivery of data frames
  - Maintaining the reliability of the communications between two computers
  - The two types of devices that function at the data link layer of the OSI model are switches and bridges.
- **The network layer** The network layer takes the frames it receives from the data link layer and organizes them into packets. Functions of the network layer include the following:
  - Physical media access control (MAC) addresses are translated into Internet Protocol (IP) addresses.
  - Routers exist at this layer.
  - Tools to check connectivity that function at the network layer include: ping, tracert, traceroute, and pathping.
- **The transport layer** The transport layer is where network packets are even further differentiated by the port number. Functions of the transport layer include the following:
  - Packets are differentiated by the Transmission Control Protocol (TCP) or User Datagram Protocol (UDP) port number they include.
  - Firewalls and proxy servers will often function at the transport layer to filter traffic.

WINDOWS TOOLS

The most common Windows tools that you should be aware of include the following:

- **Ping** Uses Internet Control Message Protocol (ICMP) echo messages to communicate with other computers. It is used to test basic TCP/IP connectivity between two computers, using either hostname or IP address. Some of the available command-line switches include *ping −t*, which will ping a specified host continuously until you stop it by typing **Ctrl + C**, and *ping −a*, which resolves IP addresses to hostnames.
- **Nslookup** Allows you to test and query the records stored in your domain naming service (DNS) server. Functions in two modes: command mode to perform a single query, or in interactive mode to perform multiple queries.
- **Tracert** Allows you to trace the path that a network packet will take from one host to another. You can use *tracert* to determine whether one of the routers

along a path, or a link between two routers, is overloaded or has failed. Some of the available command-line switches include the following:

- *tracert -d* This switch will not resolve IP addresses to hostnames.
- *tracert -h maximum_hops* This switch will indicate the maximum number of hops that tracert will use to search for a target. The default value is 30 hops.
- *tracert -w timeout* This switch indicates the amount of time each ping will wait for each reply in milliseconds. The default value is 1000 ms.

EXAM WARNING

Do not get confused between tracert and traceroute; they are essentially the same tool with different names. Tracert is used on Microsoft Windows systems and traceroute is used on other systems such as Cisco's Internetwork Operating System (IOS) as well as UNIX and Linux.

- **Arp** Allows you to view and manipulate entries in the TCP/IP arp cache. The arp cache is a list of MAC addresses for computers that have been recently contacted.
- **Ipconfig** Allows you to view the IP configuration data for all NICs installed on your local computer. Some of the available command-line switches are as follows:
  - *ipconfig/all* This switch displays information about the DNS and Windows Internet Naming Service (WINS) servers that your computer has been configured with, as well as the MAC address of each installed NIC.
  - *ipconfig/flushdns* This switch is the command to clear the DNS cache on the local computer.
  - *ipconfig/displaydns* This switch will show you the contents of the local DNS cache.
  - *ipconfig/registernds* This switch will refresh Dynamic Host Control Protocol (DHCP) leases for all NICs on the machine, and will reregister the machine's hostname and IP address with the DNS server.
- **Nbtstat** This switch displays information specifically relating to NetBIOS over TCP (NetBT). It is case sensitive. Some of the available command-line switches are as follows:
  - *nbtstat -n* This switch displays the NetBIOS names that are registered for the local computer.
  - *nbtstat –RR* This switch will release and refresh any NetBIOS name registrations on the local computer.
  - *nbtstat –R* This switch will purge and reload the current contents of the NetBIOS cache on the local machine from the LMHOSTS file that have the "#PRE" tag.
  - *nbtstat -c* This switch will display the NetBIOS name cache of NetBIOS names that have already been resolved on the local computer.
  - *nbtstat –s* This switch will display any existing NetBIOS sessions.

- **Netstat** This switch provides information about each protocol and port on a computer that is listening or that has established a connection with another computer. The *netstat* command has a number of command-line switches, for example:
    - *netstat -a* This switch displays all TCP/IP connections and listening ports on the local computer.
    - *netstat –s* This switch provides detailed statistics about the local computer's network connections.
    - *netstat -p protocol* This switch will show you the same information displayed by the –a option, restricted to a specific protocol.
    - *netstat –b* This switch displays the name of the executable that created each connection or listening port.
    - *netstat –n* This switch displays addresses and port numbers in numerical form instead of using hostnames.
  A connection listed in netstat can be in one of four states:
    - **Listening** means that a particular port is open and waiting for connections, but no active connections have been made to it.
    - **Established** means that a particular connection is active – a File Transfer Protocol (FTP) client has connected to an FTP server, a client's Web browser has connected to a World Wide Web (WWW) service, and the like.
    - **Time – Wait** means that a connection has been made, but it hasn't received any data for some time and is in the process of timing out.
    - **Close – Wait** means that an active connection is being closed.

EXAM WARNING

Make sure you understand what you are looking at when you see the output of the *netstat* command. For example, *TCP 192.168.1.3:42 192.168.1.185:3919 ESTABLISHED.* This means that the computer has ESTABLISHED or created a connection that's using the TCP between 192.168.1.3:42 and 192.168.1.185:3919, which means that the computer at IP address 192.168.1.3 is sending information using TCP port 42, and 192.168.1.185 is receiving information using port 3919.

- **Pathping** The pathping tool combines the capabilities of both tracert and ping. Pathping will calculate the following information each time it runs:
    - The amount of time it takes the ping packet to go roundtrip, which is to the destination host and back.
    - The amount of time it takes to ping each individual router.
    - The percent of ping requests that are lost at each router.
    - The percent of ping requests lost between the routers.
- **Route** The *route* command is used to manipulate and display the routing table for the local computer. The command is used to add, change, or delete routes that are defined on the local computer. To specify the route to a

remote host using the *route* command, you need to configure the following information:

- **Destination** The destination that this route statement is designed to reach.
- **Mask** This indicates the subnet mask for the route's destination.
- **Gateway** The IP address that packets will be forwarded to for this route.
- **Metric** This specifies the metric or *cost* of a particular route, from 1 to 9999. The higher the metric, the less likely the computer is to use a particular route.
- **Interface** This indicates the IP address of the NIC that should be used to reach the destination specified in this route.

Some of the available command-line switches:

- *route print* This switch displays a copy of the local computer's routing table.
- *route add* This switch adds a route to a remote network.
- *route change* This switch changes the metric of the route you just created.
- *route delete* This switch deletes a route that you've created.
- *route-f* This switch will clear any routes to destination networks that are currently in the routing table.
- *route-p* This switch will make the entry you're adding to the routing table persistent, which ensures that the route will remain in memory until you manually delete it.

- **Simple Network Management Protocol (SNMP)** SNMP is a protocol used to communicate status messages from computers and devices on your network.
  - Machines that send these messages run SNMP agent software.
  - Machines that receive the status messages run SNMP management software.
  - Allows you to audit the activities of servers, workstations, routers, bridges, intelligent hubs, and just about any network-connected device that supports SNMP agent software.
  - Uses a Management Information Base (MIB) database to describe which kinds of information should be gathered from a particular device.
  - The SNMP agent must be queried by an SNMP management system for most information.
  - A trap message is sent spontaneously by an SNMP agent to the SNMP management system when an important event occurs. SNMP trap messages are sent to UDP port 162.
  - A GET message is a request that is sent from an SNMP management system that requests information from an agent.
  - A SET message will allow the SNMP management system to write changes to an MIB, and therefore extend its information-gathering abilities.
  - SNMP GET and SET messages communicate on UDP port 161.
  - To control which machines receive SNMP trap messages, you will configure an SNMP community name and a trap destination, which is the

hostname or IP address of the computer running the SNMP management software.

LINUX TOOLS

The most common Linux tools that you should be aware of include the following:

- **Ifconfig** Used to configure the NICs installed in a Linux computer, as well as to view information about any configured interfaces.
- **Dig** Used to send name resolution queries to DNS servers to troubleshoot name resolution on a Linux-based client computer. Some of the available parameters are as follows:
  - *@server* This parameter is the fully qualified domain name (FQDN) of the computer you're querying for.
  - *-t type* This parameter specifies the type of record you're looking for, like a Mail Exchanger record (MX) or Service record (SRV) record.
  - *-f filemane* This parameter will allow dig to operate in *batch mode*, where it will perform multiple queries that it reads in from a text file.
  - *-p port* This parameter will issue a DNS query on a nonstandard port.
  - *+ domain = domainname* This parameter searches for a host using only the domain name that you specify, rather than using the search list that the Linux computer is configured with.
  - *+ [no] recursive* This parameter specifies whether to use an iterative or a recursive query. Dig queries are *recursive* by default.
  - *+ time = Time* This parameter specifies the time (in seconds) that dig should wait before deciding that a query has timed out. The default value is 5 s.

EXAM WARNING

Remember that the default DNS port is 53. DNS queries use UDP port 53, and DNS zone transfers use TCP port 53.

- **Traceroute** Allows you to trace the path that a network packet will take from one host to another. You can use traceroute to determine whether one of the routers along a path, or a link between two routers, is overloaded or has failed.

NETWARE TROUBLESHOOTING

Troubleshooting NetWare frame types:

- If NWLink is configured to use **Auto Detect** and multiple frame types are in use, then NWLink will set the Ethernet frame type to 802.2. If this is not the correct frame type, you must change it.

- You can verify that the frame type is set correctly by following these steps:
  1. Access the **Local Area Connection** dialog box on the Windows PC. Right-click the desired local area network (LAN) connection and select **Properties**.
  2. Double-click **NWLink IPX/SPX/NetBIOS Compatible Transport Protocol**.
  3. On the **General** tab, you can either verify that **Auto Detect** has been selected in the **Frame type** field, or else manually specify the frame type that should be used.

OTHER NETWORK TROUBLESHOOTING TOOLS

The most common hardware testers and tools that you should be aware of include the following:

- **Crossover cables** These are used to connect two computers or similar devices directly together, such as computers or hubs. To create a crossover cable is to rearrange the wires on one end of a standard Ethernet cable, so that they are in the following order (starting at pin 1):
  1. White/green
  2. Green
  3. White/orange
  4. White/brown
  5. Brown
  6. Orange
  7. Blue
  8. White/blue
- **Oscilloscope** An oscilloscope is used to monitor the electrical signal levels as they pass through the Ethernet cable and then display a small graph that shows how electrical signals change over time. This helps you determine the voltage and frequency of an electrical signal, and if any malfunctioning hardware components are distorting the signal.
- **Tone generator** A piece of software or a hardware device that generates the tones that are used in a telephone system, including a dial tone, busy signal, and ring tone. You can plug a tone generator into a telephone jack to determine if the jack is functioning and able to make and receive calls.
- **Cable testers** A *cable tester* is used to test for any faults or breaks in an Ethernet cable. Cable testers are designed to allow you to plug both ends of a cable into the tester. If the cable is in good condition, light emitting diode (LED) lights on the tester will light up. If there is a break in the cable (or if the wires are in the wrong order) the LED lights on the tester will not light.

IMPORTANCE OF NETWORK DOCUMENTATION

After you've done all of the necessary troubleshooting to solve a problem, documenting your troubleshooting activities is vitally important. It helps you to stay organized and perform those steps methodically. Also, when the same thing occurs again, you will be well prepared.

HOW TO USE THE OSI MODEL IN TROUBLESHOOTING

The OSI model fits into an overall troubleshooting strategy. Depending on the layer that you begin your troubleshooting, different techniques may be required to determine the root cause of the issue. The following are some of the purposes behind having a networking model:

- It provides a standard to utilize and reference, thereby helping to isolate network issues to specific layers of a protocol stack.
- It allows to identify the types of components that may be involved in an issue, thus helping in troubleshooting the problem.
- Open standards enable the consumer to patronize multiple vendors.
- Vendors produce products that can be used in various networks, including those that started out using a different vendor's products.
- The layered approach provides a logical division of responsibility, where each layer handles only the functions that are specific to that layer.
- Since the networking protocols are typically divided into layers, troubleshooting is easier because you are better able to narrow down the source of the problem to a specific layer.

Reviewing the OSI Model

The OSI model consists of seven layers, and when one computer communicates with another one, data at the sending computer is passed from one layer to the next until the final layer puts it out onto the network cable. At the receiving end, it travels back up in reverse order. Although the data travels down the layers on one side and up the layers on the other, the logical communication link is between each layer and its matching counterpart, as shown in Figure 10.1.

As the data goes down through the layers, it is *encapsulated* or enclosed within a larger unit as each layer adds its own header information. When it reaches the receiving computer, the process occurs in reverse; the information is passed upward through each layer, and as it does so, the encapsulation information is evaluated and then stripped off one layer at a time.

Establishing a Troubleshooting Strategy

The most important thing that you can do when troubleshooting is to be organized and methodical in your approach to solving problems.

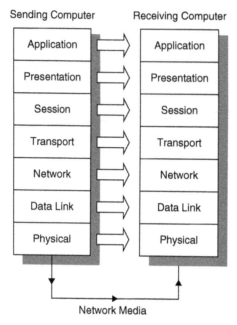

Network Media

FIGURE 10.1
Each layer of the OSI model communicates with the corresponding layer

DID YOU KNOW?

In general, you can break down the items necessary to *troubleshoot a network issue* into the following seven steps:

1. **Identify the symptoms and potential causes** Determine exactly what's wrong, and ensure that there is actually a problem. Ask questions and get very specific details on the issue. Having as much information as possible at hand will help you determine the potential causes of an issue.
2. **Identify the affected area** Is only one user having trouble, or is there an issue that's affecting an entire subnet or your entire network?
3. **Establish what has changed** Attempt to discover if anything has changed that may have caused the issue to surface. Knowing what has changed on a network will usually give you a good starting point from which you can begin the troubleshooting process.
4. **Select the most probable cause** Based on the information you gathered in the first three steps, try to determine the most likely reason why you are experiencing the particular problem. Keep in mind that your first guess might be incorrect and that there may be more than one cause for the problem.
5. **Implement an action plan and solution, including potential impact** Define the impact of any steps that you are going to take to fix the problem. Follow any change management guidance that your organization may have in place and be thoughtful of any changes you make to production systems.

6. **Test the result** Determine if your solution fixed the problem, and also examine the overall connectivity on your network to make sure that you didn't inadvertently create another issue by implementing the fix.
7. **Document the solution and process** Document the information that you gathered in each of these steps: how the problem manifested itself, the systems that were affected, the details about the solution and how you implemented it, and any side effects that came about as a result of implementing the fix.

TROUBLESHOOTING THE PHYSICAL LAYER

When troubleshooting the physical layer, you'll be most concerned with NICs, network cables, and hubs.

- Troubleshooting the NIC
  - Verify that the NIC does match the media access type
  - Verify that the NIC does have the correct connector for the cable your network uses
  - Verify that the NIC driver is properly installed and updated
- Troubleshooting cables
  - Verify that the cable meets the appropriate specifications for the network
  - Verify that the cable is not broken or damaged
  - Verify that the maximum allowable segment length for the cable type in use has not been exceeded to prevent attenuation
  - For coax networks, ensure the network is following the restrictions imposed by the 5-4-3 rule
- Troubleshooting the installation of the TCP/IP stack
  - Ensure the protocol is loaded properly by pinging the loopback address of 127.0.0.1
  - Verify that the proper addressing is configured on the NIC
- Troubleshooting repeaters and hubs
  - For active hubs, ensure that the device has power
  - Ensure that the computers' NICs are communicating with the device by checking status lights on active hubs
  - Ensure that devices are installed in accordance with the Institute of Electrical and Electronic Engineers (IEEE) specifications for the particular network architecture
  - Ensure that all ports on the device are functional by checking for a green LED lights when you attach a computer to the port through a network cable

TROUBLESHOOTING THE DATA LINK LAYER

When troubleshooting the data link layer, you'll be most concerned with bridges and switches.

- Troubleshooting bridges and switches
  - Ensure to follow the 80/20 rule, which states that 80 percent of network traffic should be local (occurring on the same side of the bridge or switch), and not more than 20 percent should cross the bridge or switch.
  - Looping can occur when there is more than one active bridge or switch on a network and the bridges and switches don't know the location of a destination computer.
  - Be sure to use the Spanning Tree Protocol when multiple bridges exist on the network.

TROUBLESHOOTING THE NETWORK LAYER

When troubleshooting the network layer, you'll be most concerned with routers and TCP/IP addressing.

- Troubleshooting routers
  - Check for configuration errors or misconfiguration issues on each router
  - Check for a routing loop by using the *tracert* or *traceroute* command
  - Verify that a route exists to the destination network
  - Check for connectivity issues between the source and destination networks, where either a router or a network link that's required has failed or gone offline.
- Troubleshooting TCP/IP addressing
  - Use the *ipconfig* command to verify that the IP address, subnet mask and default gateway, and other settings have been configured correctly
  - Use the *route* command to verify that the default gateway and other routing table entries are correct for an individual PC.

TROUBLESHOOTING THE TRANSPORT LAYER

When troubleshooting the transport layer, you'll be most concerned with TCP and UDP ports. You should be aware of the default TCP and UDP ports that are used by major applications when you're troubleshooting network issues at the transport layer. Table 10.1 illustrates some of the more common TCP applications and the ports they use, and Table 10.2 illustrates some of the more common UDP-based applications and ports.

- Troubleshooting ports
  - Use the *telnet* command to see if a particular port is listening on the destination machine.
  - Use the netstat utility to see a list of all ports that are listening on a particular machine.

Table 10.1	Well-Known TCP Ports
Port Number	**Application**
20	FTP (data)
21	FTP (control)
22	Secure Shell (SSH)
23	Telnet
25	Simple Mail Transfer Protocol (SMTP)
53	DNS
80	Hyper Text Transfer Protocol (HTTP)
88	Kerberos
110	POP3
119	Network News Transfer Protocol (NNTP)
139	NetBIOS
443	Secure sockets layer (SSL)

Table 10.2	Well-Known UDP Ports
Port Number	**Application**
7	Echo
53	DNS query
69	Trivial File Transfer Protocol (TFTP)
123	Network Time Protocol
161	SNMP

TROUBLESHOOTING THE SESSION LAYER

The functions of TCP/IP protocols from the session layer up to the application layer will often span all three layers, so it is not particularly common to perform troubleshooting that's geared only toward the session layer of the OSI model.

The most common issues you'll see at the session layer involve slow network transmissions between two computers, which is caused by one computer in a connection using a half-duplex connection instead of a full-duplex connection.

TROUBLESHOOTING THE PRESENTATION LAYER

When troubleshooting the presentation layer, the functions will often actually be performed by a protocol that you would normally think of as functioning at the application layer, so that troubleshooting will often take place with the same steps described in the application layer section. When troubleshooting gateways, an effective approach is to restart or reinstall the gateway service.

Some examples of problems you may find at the presentation layer include the following:

- An image file becomes garbled or corrupted when it's sent through e-mail from one person to another.
- E-mail messages between two different server types (for example, exchange and groupwise) become scrambled or unreadable.
- You are unable to copy or move files between two different network types, usually Microsoft and Novell, or you are unable to open a file once it's been copied.

TROUBLESHOOTING THE APPLICATION LAYER

The application layer doesn't provide services to any other OSI layer. Instead, it provides network services to user applications.

- Troubleshooting the application layer.
  - Utilize Telnet to connect to an application layer services by specifying the port that's used by the service.
  - Verify name resolution services, such as DNS and WINS are functioning properly.

Some of the common protocols that operate at the application layer are as follows:

- **FTP** FTP is used for copying files from one computer to another.
- **SNMP** SNMP provides a way to gather statistical and troubleshooting information about devices such as PCs, routers, switches, and hubs. An SNMP management system sends requests to an SNMP agent, and the information is stored in an MIB, which is a database that holds information about a networked computer.
- **Telnet** Telnet is a TCP/IP-based service that allows users to log onto a computer from a remote location, run character-mode or command-line utilities on the remote computer or device, and view files on a remote device. The Telnet server service uses TCP port 23 to listen for Telnet requests.
- **Simple Mail Transfer Protocol (SMTP)** SMTP is used for sending e-mail messages, typically across the Internet. Most e-mail client programs use SMTP for *sending* e-mail only, and either POP3 (Post Office Protocol version 3) or Internet Message Access Protocol (IMAP) for storing any messages that are received by an e-mail server. The SMTP service uses TCP port 25 to send messages using SMTP.

- **HyperText Transfer Protocol (HTTP)** HTTP allows computers to exchange files in various formats on the WWW through client software called a *Web browser*. The HTTP protocol uses TCP port 80 to send and receive information to Web servers and clients.
- **Network News Transfer Protocol (NNTP)** NNTP is used for managing messages posted to private and public newsgroups. NNTP servers provide storage of newsgroup posts, which can be downloaded by client software called a *newsreader*. The NNTP service defaults to using TCP port 119.
- **DNS** The DNS is a distributed database that is used by most of the other applications in the TCP/IP protocol suite to resolve hostnames to IP addresses. The DNS service defaults to using TCP port 53.
- **DHCP** The DHCP is used to dynamically assign TCP/IP addresses and additional configuration information to clients and servers. IP addressing information is leased by a DHCP server for a specific period of time, usually 3 days, before the lease must be renewed by the client. You can use the *ipconfig/release* and *ipconfig/renew* commands to refresh the DHCP configuration on a particular workstation.

Summary of Exam Objectives

In this chapter, we talked about the different troubleshooting tools available for you to track down and isolate connectivity problems on your network. We started by looking at the importance of having an overall framework or methodology for tackling networking issues. Before you think about the different tools available for troubleshooting, you first need to determine what the problem actually is. To do this, you need to gather as much information as possible from your users, as well as gathering information from system logs of any devices that are having the trouble.

To help you further isolate the cause of a problem that you're troubleshooting, you have a number of utilities available in the Windows and Linux operating systems. To test basic TCP/IP connectivity between two hosts, you can use the *ping* command. You can also use the *tracert* command on a Windows computer or *traceroute* on Linux to view the actual path that network traffic takes between two hosts. On Windows Vista, XP and 2000, you can use the *pathping* command, which combines the features of *ping* and *tracert* into a single utility.

To troubleshoot name resolution issues, you can use *nslookup* on a Windows computer and *dig* on Linux. These commands will allow you to verify that your DNS servers are functioning properly and have the correct information with which to answer client queries. For Windows-based computers that rely on NetBIOS, you can use the *nbtstat* command to troubleshoot NetBIOS name resolution. To troubleshoot the physical components of your network, including network cables and wall jacks, you should also be familiar with the purpose of an Ethernet crossover cable, as well as cable testers that are designed to test Ethernet cables for flaws or breaks.

Following an organized set of troubleshooting steps allows you to organize the troubleshooting process and makes it less likely that you will overlook something important along the way. To make a diagnosis or analysis of the information, you must organize it in a logical manner. Solutions, once formulated, should be prioritized according to cost, time involved, longevity, and long-term effect on performance.

Top Five Toughest Questions

1. Examine the *tracert* output shown in Figure 10.2. What is a possible explanation for the "Request timed out" values shown? Choose all that apply.
   A. The router at hop 10 is down
   B. The router at that hop is configured to drop ping packets
   C. There has been an incorrect DNS resolution, and the wrong router is being contacted
   D. The maximum hop count has been reached, so all other hops beyond it will show *Request timed out*
2. You are the network administrator for a network who employs a Windows 2003 server and 30 Windows XP Professional workstations. The Windows 2003 server runs the DHCP service to provide TCP/IP configuration information to the Windows XP clients. You receive a call from one of your users stating that he is unable to browse any internal network resources or

```
Administrator: Command Prompt
C:\>tracert www.microsoft.com

Tracing route to lb1.www.ms.akadns.net [207.46.19.190]
over a maximum of 30 hops:

  1     1 ms     1 ms     1 ms  dns.the3bears.com [192.168.1.1]
  2    19 ms     7 ms     7 ms  cpe-071-075-000-001.carolina.res.rr.com [71.75.0.1]
  3     9 ms     8 ms     8 ms  24.93.65.165
  4    16 ms     7 ms    34 ms  srp0-0.chrlncsa-rtr1.carolina.rr.com [24.93.67.161]
  5    14 ms    25 ms    14 ms  ge-2-2-0.rlghncrdc-pop1.southeast.rr.com [24.93.64.171]
  6    29 ms    21 ms    29 ms  ae-3-0.cr0.dca10.tbone.rr.com [66.109.6.80]
  7    20 ms    25 ms    22 ms  ae-0-0.cr0.dca20.tbone.rr.com [66.109.6.31]
  8    35 ms    29 ms    43 ms  ae-3-0.cr0.nyc30.tbone.rr.com [66.109.6.29]
  9    31 ms    61 ms    29 ms  ae-1-0.pr0.nyc20.tbone.rr.com [66.109.6.163]
 10     *        *        *     Request timed out.
 11     *        *        *     Request timed out.
 12     *        *        *     Request timed out.
 13     *        *        *     Request timed out.
 14     *        *        *     Request timed out.
 15     *        *        *     Request timed out.
 16     *        *        *     Request timed out.
 17     *        *        *     Request timed out.
 18     *        *        *     Request timed out.
 19     *        *        *     Request timed out.
 20     *        *        *     Request timed out.
 21     *        *        *     Request timed out.
 22     *        *        *     Request timed out.
 23     *        *        *     Request timed out.
 24     *        *        *     Request timed out.
 25     *        *        *     Request timed out.
 26     *        *        *     Request timed out.
 27     *        *        *     Request timed out.
 28     *        *        *     Request timed out.
 29     *        *        *     Request timed out.
 30     *        *        *     Request timed out.

Trace complete.

C:\>
```

FIGURE 10.2
Sample *tracert* output

Internet Web sites. Other users on the same subnet are able to browse without difficulty. You run the *ipconfig* command on the problem workstation and see the following output:

Windows IP Configuration
Host Name   : IBM-A38375FF22E
Primary Dns Suffix   :
Node Type   : Hybrid
IP Routing Enabled   : No
WINS Proxy Enabled   : No
Ethernet adapter Wireless
Network Connection:
Connection-specific DNS Suffix   :
Description   : Intel(R) PRO/Wireless 2200BG
                                     Network Connection
Physical Address   : 00-1E-25-1A-D3-5A
Dhcp Enabled   : Yes
Autoconfiguration Enabled   : Yes
IP Address   : 169.254.1.96
Subnet Mask   : 255.255.0.0
Default Gateway   :
DHCP Server   :
DNS Servers   :
Lease Obtained   : Tuesday, March 29, 2005 1:00:10 PM
Lease Expires   : Wednesday, March 30, 2005
                                     1:00:10 PM

Based on this output, why is this workstation unable to browse any network resources?
A. The default gateway is unavailable
B. The workstation could not contact a DHCP server
C. The workstation is configured with the incorrect default gateway
D. The workstation's DHCP lease has expired

3. You are the network administrator for a large pharmaceutical company that has over 1000 workstations. To simplify TCP/IP configuration for these numerous clients, you installed a DHCP server over a year ago to automatically configure your clients with an IP address, as well as the following common configuration information:

Subnet Mask: 255.255.0.0
Default Gateway: 172.16.0.1
DNS Servers: 172.16.0.100
             172.16.0.101

As part of a recent network redesign, you had to change the default gateway used by your clients to a different IP address: 172.16.1.1. You made the necessary change on the DHCP server, and most of your clients were updated automatically. After you make this change, you receive a call from one user who no longer is able to browse the Internet. You examine the TCP/IP configuration of her LAN connection (see Figure 10.3).

How can you configure this workstation with the correct default gateway information? (Each choice represents a complete solution. Choose two.)

A. Delete the manually configured information and select **Obtain an IP address** automatically

B. Run *ipconfig/renew* from the command prompt

C. Manually update the IP address of the default gateway

D. Run *ipconfig/release* from the command prompt

Internet Protocol (TCP/IP) Properties   [?] [X]

General

You can get IP settings assigned automatically if your network supports this capability. Otherwise, you need to ask your network administrator for the appropriate IP settings.

○ Obtain an IP address automatically

◉ Use the following IP address:

IP address:	172 . 16 . 0 . 135
Subnet mask:	255 . 255 . 0 . 0
Default gateway:	172 . 16 . 0 . 1

○ Obtain DNS server address automatically

◉ Use the following DNS server addresses:

Preferred DNS server:	172 . 16 . 0 . 100
Alternate DNS server:	172 . 16 . 0 . 101

[Advanced...]

[OK]   [Cancel]

FIGURE 10.3
Sample TCP/IP configuration

4. You are the administrator of the network shown in Figure 10.4. The firewall in the exhibit was installed by an outside consultant a few weeks ago. Once a month, one of your company's employees needs to access the FTP site of one of your company's business partners, ftp.airplanes.com to download large PDF files containing product marketing information. You receive a help desk call from this employee, stating that he is now unable to access this FTP site. The last time he performed this task was before the firewall was installed, and he says that it worked fine then. You are able to ping the ftp.airplanes.com DNS name, and you can access www.airplanes.com, which is located on the same physical machine. What is the best way to restore this employee's access to the ftp.airplanes.com FTP site?

A. Configure a firewall rule allowing traffic to TCP ports 20 and 21

B. Configure a firewall rule allowing traffic to TCP ports 25 and 110

C. Configure a firewall rule allowing all TCP traffic to this employee's workstation

D. Configure a firewall rule allowing traffic to TCP ports 80 and 443

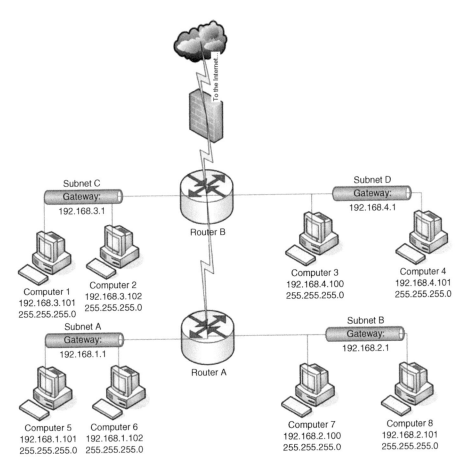

FIGURE 10.4
Sample network topology

5. Your e-mail server is having network connectivity problems. You have replaced the NIC and reconfigured the IP address. The last step that you take is to start the e-mail services, and all services have now started successfully without generating error messages. Which of the following actions will allow you to verify that the e-mail services are successfully accepting inbound e-mail?
   A. Telnet from a client machine to port 25 on the e-mail server
   B. Telnet from a client machine to port 23 on the e-mail server
   C. Use POP3 to create an e-mail queue and validate that e-mail passes through it successfully
   D. Use IMAP4 to send Internet e-mail to the server

Answers

1. Correct answers and explanations: **A** and **B**. Answer **A** is correct because when a router is down it is possible that a *Request timed out* can be the response listed. Answer **B** is correct because if a router is configured not to respond to ping attempts, *Request timed out* will be displayed and none of the routers which should receive the packets after that one will get them. When a *tracert* command is issued, a ping is being sent to each hop along the route. If ping is blocked by a specific router, then no response is received and the request will time out resulting in the *Request timed out* displayed above.

   Incorrect answers and explanations: **C** and **D**. Answer **C** is incorrect because the next hop is not determined by DNS resolution. The next hop is determined by the previous hop. If a router is misconfigured, the wrong path can take place, but this would not be attributed to DNS. Answer **D** is incorrect, because the maximum hop count is 30, and tracert simply ends when it reaches the maximum hop count. It does not display *Request timed out* when the maximum hop count is reached.

2. Correct Answers & Explanations: **B**. Answer **B** is correct, because the workstation is displaying a 169.254.1.96 IP address, which is an APIPA address. APIPA is short for Automatic Private IP Address and covers a range of 169.254.0.0 through 169.254.255.254. An address from this range is automatically assigned to a machine when it is configured to utilize DHCP, but it is not able to contact a DHCP server. Typically when a machine is assigned an APIPA address it is not able to connect to with the rest of the network, since the rest of the network will most likely be utilizing a different addressing scheme. In very small business networks and home network environment is it possible to rely on APIPA for addressing. APIPA does not configure variables such as a gateway, so in most corporate environments where routers exist APIPA isn't appropriate for network configurations.

   Incorrect Answers & Explanations: **A**, **C**, and **D**. Answer **A** is incorrect, because a default gateway is never configured when an APIPA address has been assigned. Answer **C** is incorrect, because the workstation does not have a gateway value configured; it has an APIPA address configured, which never has an accompanying gateway value. Answer **D** is incorrect, because when a workstation's DHCP lease has expired it will attempt to renew its existing IP address. It is only is if is unsuccessful in renewal that it will be forced to abandon the currently issued IP address. It will then issue an APIPA address instead.

3. Correct answers and explanations: **A** and **C**. Answer **A** is correct because by changing the configuration to obtain an IP address automatically, the machine will connect to the DHCP server to receive an IP address and also receive the configured options which include the new default gateway value. Answer **C** is correct because by manually updating the IP address of the default gateway on the client machine, it will be able to connect to the correct default gateway.

Incorrect answers and explanations: **B** and **D**. Answer **B** is incorrect because an *ipconfig/renew* command will force a client to attempt renewal of its DHCP address. Since this client machine is configured with a static IP address, issuing this command will not have an effect, and will not cause the client machine to receive the correct default gateway from the DHCP server. Answer **D** is incorrect because *ipconfig/release* command will force a client to release its current DHCP address. Since this client machine is configured with a static IP address, issuing this command will not have an effect and will not cause the client machine to release a DHCP address since it doesn't have one. Also, since it is configured with a static IP address, this command will not cause the client to receive the correct default gateway from the DHCP server.

4. Correct answers and explanations: **A**. Answer **A** is correct because ports 20 and 21 are used for FTP traffic. By configuring the firewall to allow FTP traffic to pass through, the user will be able to transfer the files required successfully.

Incorrect answers and explanations: **B**, **C**, and **D**. Answer **B** is incorrect because ports 25 and 110 are not utilized for FTP. Port 25 is utilized by SMTP and 110 is utilized by POP3. Answer **C** is incorrect because allowing all TCP traffic to the user's workstation when only FTP is required is an unnecessary change, which leaves the machine vulnerable. Answer **D** is incorrect because ports 80 and 443 are not utilized for FTP. Port 80 is utilized by HTTP and port 443 is utilized by Secure HTTP (HTTPS).

5. Correct answers and explanations: **A**. Answer **A** is correct because by the *telnet* command can be used to verify that a port on a particular machine is open. Issuing the *telnet* command on port 25 will validate that the SMTP services which are responsible for inbound e-mail are up and functioning.

Incorrect answers and explanations: **B**, **C**, and **D**. Answer **B** is incorrect because port 23 is the default telnet port and you cannot determine if e-mail services are functioning correctly by telenetting to port 23. Answer **C** is incorrect because POP3 is a protocol used to receive e-mail from server to a client. It is not used to create or validate queue. Answer **D** is incorrect because IMAP4 is a protocol used to receive e-mail from server to a client.

Access Determines who can use the network and how, and if features of the network are available for private or public use.

Access Control Lists (ACLs) A list of permissions that specifies access to an object.

Application Level Firewall A firewall that understands the data at the application level and functions at the application, presentation, and session layers of the OSI network model.

Application Program Interface (API) This layer of Microsoft's Windows model is the interface through which developers can access the network infrastructure services such as various application layer protocols.

Application Server A client/server role that allows clients to run certain programs on the server and enables multiple users to utilize common applications across the network.

Authentication Server Used to verify the supplicant port access entity (PAE), the authentication server decides whether or not the supplicant is authorized to access the authenticator.

Authenticator PAE An entity that enforces authentication before allowing access to resources located off of that port.

Bandwidth A measurement of the amount of data that can be passed over a cable in a given amount of time.

Bayonet–Neill–Concelman (BNC) A type of locking connector used to terminate coaxial cables.

Bridge A network device that has the ability to forward packets of data based on **Media Access Control** (MAC) addresses. A bridge can look at a packet of data and determine the source and destination involved in the transfer of packets.

Broadcast Messages Messages that are sent out to all of the nodes in a broadcast domain.

Cable Testers Tools that can analyze the capability of a cable to carry signals.

Cabling A term that can refer to the act of installing the cable and the work performed before installation of a network begins.

Carrier Protocol The protocol used by the network (Internet Protocol [IP] on the Internet) that the information is traveling over.

Channel Service Unit/Data Service Unit (CSU/DSU) A device that takes a signal from a digital medium and multiplexes it.

Coaxial Cable A cable that contains a single copper wire at the center of the cable core that is used to carry the signals. Coaxial cable is surrounded by layers of insulation that protect the wire and its transmissions. There are two coaxial types: Thinnet (10Base2) and Thicknet (10Base5).

Content Switch A network device that uses layers 4 to 7 of the OSI Model, and rather than looking at the individual packets being transmitted, it can use sessions to transmit data between machines.

Crossover Cable A twisted-pair cable with two wires crossed that is used to connect two computers to each other directly without the use of a hub.

Crosstalk Crosstalk occurs when the electromagnetic field of one wire interferes with the transmission of data along another wire.

DARPA Model The Defense Advanced Research Projects Agency's four-layer architecture that provides a foundation for internetworking. This architecture is also referred to as the Department of Defense (DoD) model.

Database Server A client/server role that allows authorized clients to view, modify, and/or delete data in a common database.

Default Gateway A router that is used to forward data packets with a destination IP address not on the local subnet.

Demarc A term used to describe where the provider's equipment ends and the private network begins.

Demilitiarized Zone (DMZ) A neutral network segment where systems accessible to the public Internet are housed, and which offers some basic levels of protection against attacks.

Denial-of-Service Attack A denial of service occurs when an attacker has engaged most of the resources that a host or network has available, rendering it unavailable to legitimate users.

Dynamic Host Configuration Protocol (DHCP) A broadcast-based protocol that is used to automatically assign TCP/IP addressing information to computers.

DNS Server A service that maps IP addresses to host names.

Dual-Homed Host Firewall A firewall that consists of a single computer with two physical network interfaces.

Eavesdropping The act of listening to data being sent over the wire without actually piercing the cable.

Electromagnetic Interference (EMI) A low-voltage, low-current, high-frequency signal that comes from an outside source that can interfere with the electronic signals transmitted through cables.

Encapsulating Protocol The protocol, such as Point-to-Point Tunneling Protocol (PPTP), Layer 2 Tunneling Protocol (L2TP), IP security (IPSec), or secure shell (SSH), that is wrapped around the original data.

Ethernet The standard speed of 10 Mbps, coaxial, or twisted pair cable.

Extensible Authentication Protocol over LAN (EAPoL) 802.11i defines a standard for encapsulating EAP messages, so that they can be handled directly by a LAN MAC service.

Extensible Authentication Protocol over Wireless (EAPoW) When EAPoL messages are encapsulated over 802.11 wireless frames, they are known as *EAPoW*.

Fast Ethernet The standard speed of 100 Mbps, coaxial, or twisted pair cable.

File Server A client/server role that allows clients to save data to folders on its hard drive.

Firewall A device that protects a secure internal network from a public insecure network. Firewalls have the ability to control the traffic that is sent from an external network, such as the Internet, to an internal network or local computer.

Full Duplex A term that refers to data traveling in both directions simultaneously.

Gateway A bridge connecting two dissimilar systems.

Gigabit Ethernet The standard speed of 1 Gbps, twisted-pair or fiber-optic cable.

Half Duplex A term that refers to data traveling both ways, but in only one direction at a time.

Hardware Loopback Adapter A tool that provides a way to test the ports on a system without having to connect to an external device.

Hub A device that passes data to other computers or networks. Hubs, or concentrators, are central devices where network cabling is connected. Multiple cables connect into the hub, providing a method for data to be passed from one cable to another.

Integrated Services Digital Network (ISDN) A system of digital telephone connections that enables data to be transmitted simultaneously end to end.

Intrusion Detection System (IDS) A device designed to inspect and detect the kinds of traffic or network behavior patterns that match known attack signatures or that suggest potential unrecognized attacks may be incipient or in progress.

Load Balancer A device that will distribute connection load between multiple devices in your environment that are serving the same function.

Local Connector (LC) A connector used with fiber-optic cabling.

Logical Link Control (LLC) A sublayer of the data link layer of the OSI model. The LLC provides the logic for the data link layer.

Man-in-the-Middle Through Rogue Access Points Interception of network communications through deployment of an access point (AP) with enough strength so that the end users may not be able to tell which AP is the authorized one that they should be using.

Mechanical Transfer Registered Jack (MTRJ) A connector used with fiber-optic cabling.

Media Cables or wireless technologies that carry the data across the network.

Media Access Control (MAC) A sublayer of the data link layer of the OSI model. It provides control for accessing the transmission medium.

Media Converter A device used when you have two types of dissimilar media that need to be converged.

Multifunction Devices A device (for example, a network printer or server) that has the capability to do more than just a single function.

Multiport Bridge It is another name for a switch. Switches can perform the same functions as a bridge, which can connect two (local area networks) LANs together or segment a large one into two smaller ones.

Multilayer Switch A switch that uses a combination of switching and routing. A multilayer switch (also called a Layer 3 switch) works by utilizing switching tables and switching algorithms to determine how to send data through MAC addressing from host-to-host or device-to-device.

Network Device Interface Specification (NDIS) The layer of Microsoft's Windows model that maps to the data link layer of the OSI model and the network interface layer of the Defense Advanced Research Projects Agency (DARPA) model.

Network Attached Storage (NAS) Devices that are dedicated to providing storage of data on the network. NAS uses hard disks for storage, but instead of being installed on a server, the storage device is accessed through its own network address.

Network Adapter A device that allows computers to transmit and receive data across the network.

Network Interface Card (NIC) A device that allows computers to transmit and receive data across the network. A NIC can also be referred to as a network adapter card or network card.

Network A system that interconnects computers and other devices and provides a method of communication and the ability to share data.

Network Hijacking Usage of a legitimate IP address or MAC address by an unauthorized device, oftentimes, resulting in the redirection of legitimate data packets to the unauthorized device. This is also called *spoofing*.

Network Model Determines the levels of security that are available to the network and the components needed to connect the computers together.

Network Monitor A tool that monitors traffic on the network and displays the packets that have been transmitted across the network.

Network Operating Systems (NOS) Softwares such as Windows, NetWare, or Linux that may be used for a server, which is a computer that provides services to numerous computers, and/or installed on computers that are used by individual users of the network.

Network Type Defines the size of the network and its scale within a geographical area.

Open Systems Interconnection (OSI) Model A seven-layered framework used as the model for distributed communications that was formed by the International Organization for Standardization in 1977.

Oscilloscope A cable troubleshooting tool that can determine if there are shorts, crimps, or attenuation in the cable.

Packet Level Firewall A form of screening router that examines packets based upon filters that are set up at the network and transport layers of the OSI network model.

Passenger Protocol The original data being carried.

Peer-to-Peer Network A simple type of network in which the computers on it act as equals, with each workstation providing access to resources and data.

Port A single point of connection to a network.

Port Access Entity (PAE) An entity that controls the algorithms and protocols associated with the authentication mechanisms for a port.

Print Server A client/server role that redirects print jobs from clients to specific printers.

Protocol Sets of rules that control how the data is sent between computers.

Protocol Analyzers A tool that monitors traffic on the network and displays the packets that have been transmitted across the network.

Proxy Server A server that performs a function on behalf of another system, typically browser-based requests to and from the Internet.

Radio Frequency Interference (RFI) RFI is caused by electromagnetic radiation in the radiofrequency range generated by radio and television broadcast towers, microwave satellite dishes, appliances, and furnaces.

Router A device that routes data packets across a network by opening the packet and making routing decisions based on the contents.

Registered Jack (RJ) A connector used with twisted-pair cables.

Repeater A network device that will take a signal that may be weakening and regenerate it to its original strength so that the data doesn't corrupt as it travels over long distances.

Simplex A term used to refer to data moving in a single direction.

Smart Jack A term used to describe the box (or case) and internal cards (and other hardware) where you terminate your router or switching device to get access to the lease line company's circuit.

Switch A switch stores Layer 2 address information (MAC addresses) regarding each host connected to it.

Screened Host Firewall A firewall that has a screening router placed between the gateway host and the public network.

Screened Subnet Firewall A firewall configuration that isolates the internal network from the public network.

Sniffing The electronic form of eavesdropping on the communications that computers transmit across networks.

Spoofing Usage of a legitimate IP address or MAC address by an unauthorized device oftentimes resulting in the redirection of legitimate data packets to the unauthorized device. This is also called *network hijacking*.

Standard Connector (SC) A connector used with fiber-optic cabling.

Straight Tip (ST) A connector used with fiber-optic cabling.

Subnet A network segment.

Subnet Mask A 32-bit number that is to shield or mask certain bits.

Supernetting The process of combining smaller networks into one larger network.

Supplicant PAE An entity that tries to access the services that are allowed by the authenticator.

Transmission Control Protocol/Internet Protocol (TCP/IP) A suite of protocols that provides the functionality specified in the OSI model using the four related layers of the DoD model: network interface, Internet, host-to-host, and application.

Transport Driver Interface (TDI) This layer of Microsoft's Windows model provides a portal into the transport protocols for kernel mode components such as servers and redirectors. It acts as the gateway between the transport layer and the session layer in the OSI model, providing a common interface developers can use to access both transport and session layer functionality.

Thicknet (10Base5) Cable that is 0.5 in. thick. It is often used to connect endpoints to the backbone of a network.

Thinnet (10Base2) Cable that is 0.25 in. thick. It is often used as a network backbone since the thicker cable allows for increased speeds and distances.

Time Domain Reflectometer (TDR) A cable troubleshooting tool that uses an electronic pulse, which travels down the cable until it is reflected back.

Tone Generator A cable troubleshooting tool used to perform tests that will aid in the identification of wires during the wire-tracing process.

Topology The shape of the network that defines how the network is designed and describes how computers are connected together.

Transceiver This term is short for a transmitter-receiver, a component of a NIC that transmits and receives electrical signals across the transmission media.

Virtual Local Area Networks (VLANs) VLANs allow network administrators to divide the network by designating certain switch ports as part of a logical network.

Virtual Private Network (VPN) VPNs provide users with a secure method of connectivity through a public internetwork, such as the Internet, into the internal network of an organization.

Wide Area Network (WAN) A computer network covering a wide geographical area, including more than one remote location.

Wireless Network A network that requires minimal cabling, as data is transmitted over the air using wireless adapters and wireless routers.

Wire Map Tester It is used to test for opens, shorts, and crossed pairs.

Wiretapping Gaining physical access to a network cable and cutting or piercing the cable so that the wires inside the cable can be accessed and then spliced or tapped.

Index